Bourne Klein

SOUTH OF MIDNIGHT
GAME GUIDE 2025

Dominate the Dark Fantasy World with Expert Strategies, Powerful Builds, and Exclusive Tips for Every Player: From Newcomers to Pro Gamers.

CHAPTER 1: INTRODUCTION TO SOUTH OF MIDNIGHT

The World of South of Midnight

Welcome to the hauntingly beautiful world of *South of Midnight*, where folklore meets fantasy in a rich tapestry of mystery and wonder. Set against the backdrop of the American South, this game weaves a tale as thick as the bayou mist a place where ancient legends breathe, and every shadow tells a story. From the moment you step into this world, you are not just a player; you are a traveler, an adventurer navigating the thin veil between reality and the supernatural.

A Land Steeped in Myth and Mystery

The world of *South of Midnight* isn't just a setting; it's a living, breathing character. Every gnarled tree, crumbling ruin, and moonlit swamp carries the weight of untold stories. This is a place where folklore comes alive where voodoo myths and Southern Gothic horror converge to create an atmosphere that is both eerie and enchanting. As you traverse the game's open world, you'll encounter spectral figures, cursed landmarks, and secrets older than time itself.

What makes this world so captivating is its blend of the familiar and the fantastical. One moment you're walking through a sleepy town with peeling paint and rusted street signs; the next, you're face-to-face with a creature straight out of legend. Every location feels grounded yet otherworldly, drawing you deeper into the narrative with every step.

Regions and Environments

South of Midnight is divided into distinct regions, each with its own unique atmosphere and challenges. Whether you're wading through the swamps of Cypress Hollow or exploring the decaying streets of Ember Grove, the game constantly keeps you on edge not with jump scares, but with a sense of dread that creeps under your skin.

- **Cypress Hollow:** A murky swamp where the trees seem to whisper your name. The air is thick with fog, and the water ripples unnaturally. This is where many legends begin, and where few dares to tread.

- **Ember Grove:** Once a thriving town, now a decaying relic of the past. Ghost stories are more than bedtime tales here they're warnings.

- **The Forgotten Reach:** A place untouched by time, where ancient ruins hold the keys to powerful secrets. It's beautiful, but dangerous to the unprepared.

- **The Midnight Coast:** A desolate shoreline where the waves carry more than just driftwood. This is where the boundaries between worlds are at their thinnest.

Each of these regions offers more than just stunning visuals; they challenge you to adapt, survive, and uncover the truth hidden in the shadows.

The Lore That Binds It All

In *South of Midnight*, lore isn't something you read in dusty tomes it's woven into every aspect of the game. NPCs speak in hushed tones about "the old ones" and "things best left undisturbed." Strange symbols etched into stone walls beg to be deciphered, while scattered letters and journal entries reveal the desperate last words of those who came before you.

But it's not just about reading the lore; it's about experiencing it. From cursed objects that whisper their tragic backstories to spectral encounters that linger long after they're gone, every piece of the world invites you to dig deeper. The game rewards curiosity, encouraging you to explore every dark corner and listen to every unsettling sound.

A World That Reacts to You

What makes *South of Midnight* truly special is how alive the world feels. Your choices matter not just in the grand, game-changing decisions but in the small moments too. Help a stranded traveler in the swamp, and you might gain a powerful ally. Ignore the warnings of a ghostly figure, and you could find yourself cursed. The world remembers your actions, and its inhabitants respond accordingly.

Day and night cycles bring a dynamic element to exploration. By day, the world feels eerie but manageable; by night, the darkness breathes new life into old terrors. Certain creatures only emerge under the cover of darkness, and safe havens become few and far between.

Why This World Matters

The world of *South of Midnight* isn't just a setting, it's a story in itself. It pulls you in with its haunting beauty and keeps you hooked with its rich lore and dynamic gameplay. Whether you're wandering the moonlit marshes or uncovering the truth behind the town's forgotten tragedies, every moment feels purposeful.

This isn't a world you simply pass through; it's a world you survive, shape, and, if you're lucky, come to understand. In *South of Midnight*, the midnight hour isn't just a time it's a place. And once you enter, you may never want to leave.

Story and Setting Overview

In *South of Midnight*, the line between reality and myth is razor-thin. Set in the heart of the American South, this game offers a dark and captivating narrative steeped in Southern Gothic folklore. It is a tale of survival, redemption, and the haunting power of secrets left to fester. From the decaying small towns to the murky bayous, every inch of this world has a story to tell and it's not always a pleasant one.

The Premise

You play as **Cal Morgan**, a drifter with a troubled past and a knack for finding trouble where it hides. After receiving a mysterious letter about a long-lost family heirloom tied to a forgotten town called **Hollow's Edge**, you set out on a journey that quickly spirals into something far more sinister. What starts as a simple quest for answers soon becomes a battle against the dark forces that lurk in the shadows.

But this is no typical hero's journey. In *South of Midnight*, not all monsters are born some are made. As you uncover the town's dark history, you'll be forced to confront not only the creatures of the night but also the ghosts of your own past.

A Setting Like No Other

The game is set in an alternate version of the American South, where folklore isn't just a bedtime story it's a reality woven into everyday life. The setting is a masterful blend of Southern Gothic aesthetics and dark fantasy elements. Rusted pickup trucks sit abandoned next to ancient stone totems. Creaking porches groan under the weight of secrets, and the air is thick with the scent of swamp water and old magic.

Key Locations:

- **Hollow's Edge:** A once-thriving town now drowning in its own history. Its people are tight-lipped, its streets are haunted by whispers, and its secrets run deeper than its roots.

- **The Wraithwood:** A dense forest that locals avoid after dark. It's said that those who venture too deep never return or worse, they come back... different.

- **The Drowned Fields:** Once fertile farmland, now a flooded expanse where the dead do not rest. Strange lights hover over the water at night, and something ancient stirs beneath the surface.

- **The Midnight Crossroads:** A place where deals are made, and souls are lost. It's said that if you stand there at midnight, you can bargain with something older than time.

Themes and Narrative Depth

At its core, *South of Midnight* is more than just a game about fighting monsters it's a story about the weight of history and the price of ignoring it. The game explores themes of guilt, redemption, and the cyclical nature of trauma. Many of the characters you meet carry burdens of their own, and your interactions with them can shape not only their fates but also the course of the entire story.

You'll face moral choices that blur the line between right and wrong. Do you help the vengeful spirit seeking justice for her untimely death, even if it means harming the living? Do you trust the charming drifter who offers you help, knowing he may be hiding a darker agenda? Every decision you make ripples through the world, shaping the outcome in ways both subtle and profound.

A Living, Breathing Narrative

The beauty of *South of Midnight* lies in its ability to make the world feel alive. Dialogue choices, exploration, and even how you choose to approach certain missions can alter the game's narrative in surprising ways. Side quests aren't just filler content they provide deeper insight into the world and its people, offering emotional depth that makes the story resonate long after the credits roll.

The setting itself tells a story. A boarded-up church hints at a community that lost its faith. A rusted locket found in the mud reveals the tragic end of a forbidden love. Environmental storytelling is everywhere, rewarding players who take the time to explore every dark corner.

Why the Story Matters

In *South of Midnight*, the story isn't just something you watch unfold it's something you live. It's a journey through loss, fear, and ultimately, hope. The setting is more than just a backdrop; it is a reflection of the characters who inhabit it, including you.

This is a world where the past never truly dies, and the choices you make determine whether you break the cycle or become another forgotten ghost. Whether you're drawn to the rich lore, the haunting atmosphere, or the complex characters, one thing is certain once you step into *South of Midnight*, you won't leave unchanged.

Main Characters and Factions

The heart of *South of Midnight* beats through its characters and factions a diverse cast of heroes, villains, and morally grey figures who breathe life into the game's rich narrative. Every character you encounter carries a history as heavy as the Southern air, and every faction has motives buried deeper than the roots of the oldest cypress trees. In this world, alliances are fragile, trust is a luxury, and survival often comes at a cost.

Main Characters

Cal Morgan The Drifter with a Past

You step into the worn boots of **Cal Morgan**, a lone wanderer with a haunted past. Orphaned young and hardened by years on the road, Cal is no stranger to the darkness both outside and within. What sets Cal apart is the player's ability to shape their personality through choices. Whether you play as a ruthless survivor or a compassionate protector, Cal's journey is one of self-discovery, redemption, and facing the consequences of past actions.

- **Strengths:** Adaptive, resourceful, skilled in combat.

- **Weaknesses:** Haunted by guilt, struggles with trust.

- **Motivation:** To uncover the truth behind their family's dark legacy.

Lucille Hartley The Keeper of Secrets

A sharp-tongued, no-nonsense woman who runs the **Last Light Tavern**, Lucille knows more than she lets on. She serves drinks by day and information by night, acting as the unofficial historian of Hollow's Edge. If you want answers, Lucille has them but they don't come cheap.

- **Strengths:** Knowledgeable, well-connected.

- **Weaknesses:** Distrustful of outsiders.

- **Motivation:** To protect her town's secrets at any cost.

The Midnight Man: The Deal Maker

Every legend has a monster, and in *South of Midnight*, that monster wears a smile. The **Midnight Man** is a mysterious figure who appears when the clock strikes twelve, offering deals too good to be true. But every gift has a price, and the Midnight Man never forgets a debt.

- **Strengths:** Manipulative, nearly omniscient.

- **Weaknesses:** Bound by the rules of the crossroads.

- **Motivation:** To collect souls and uphold the balance.

Eli Wade The: Cursed Hunter

Once the town's most respected hunter, Eli is now a shadow of the man he used to be. Cursed by a creature he failed to kill, Eli roams the swamps, half-man and half-beast, struggling to keep his humanity intact. He may be your greatest ally or your worst enemy.

- **Strengths:** Expert tracker, unmatched strength.

- **Weaknesses:** Uncontrollable rage under the full moon.

- **Motivation:** To break the curse before it consumes him.

Factions

The Hollow's Edge Militia

What started as a group of townsfolk defending their home has turned into something far more sinister. The **Hollow's Edge Militia** keeps the peace through fear, and they don't take kindly to outsiders meddling in their affairs. With ties to dark forces they barely understand, they blur the line between protectors and oppressors.

- **Allies:** Loyal townsfolk, opportunistic mercenaries.

- **Enemies:** Anyone who questions their authority.

- **Motivation:** To maintain control at any cost.

The Circle of Thorns

A secretive cult devoted to the old gods that dwell beneath the swamp. They believe that by offering blood sacrifices, they can gain power and immortality. Their influence runs deeper than most realize, and their members walk among the town disguised as ordinary citizens.

- **Allies:** Dark entities, cursed creatures.

- **Enemies:** Anyone who stands in the way of their rituals.

- **Motivation:** To awaken the old gods and claim eternal power.

The Swampkin

Neither fully human nor fully beast, the **Swampkin** are the native creatures of the Drowned Fields. They are ancient guardians, bound to the land and its magic. While they are not inherently hostile, they do not suffer trespassers lightly. Earn their trust, and you may gain powerful allies. Cross them, and you may not leave the swamp alive.

- **Allies:** The natural world, ancient magic.

- **Enemies:** Poachers, cultists, and destructive outsiders.

- **Motivation:** To protect the land from corruption.

The Wanderers

A ragtag group of nomads, traders, and exiles who travel the backroads of *South of Midnight*. They hold no loyalty to any town or faction, but they have eyes and ears everywhere. If you need supplies, information, or a place to hide, the Wanderers might help for the right price.

- **Allies:** No one and everyone.

- **Enemies:** Those who betray their trust.

- **Motivation:** Survival through neutrality and trade.

What to Expect from This Guide

This guide is more than just a walkthrough it's your ultimate companion to mastering *South of Midnight*. Whether you're a casual gamer looking to explore the rich lore or a seasoned player seeking advanced strategies, this guide offers something for everyone. Here's what you can expect as you journey through the pages ahead:

Comprehensive Walkthroughs

From the first steps in Hollow's Edge to the final confrontation with the Midnight Man, we cover every mission, side quest, and boss fight in meticulous detail. With tips on how to approach combat, exploration, and decision-making, you'll never feel lost.

Expert Strategies for Every Playstyle

Whether you prefer to tackle enemies head-on or take a stealthier approach, this guide offers tailored strategies for all playstyles. You'll learn how to build powerful character builds, manage resources efficiently, and adapt to the game's dynamic environments.

Lore and World-Building Insights

South of Midnight is a game rich with lore, and we've left no stone unturned. From the origins of the Midnight Crossroads to the tragic past of Hollow's Edge, you'll gain a deeper appreciation of the game's storytelling and world-building.

Secrets, Collectibles, and Hidden Content

If you're a completionist, this guide is your best friend. We highlight every collectible, hidden location, and Easter egg, ensuring you don't miss a single detail.

Achievements, Trophies, and Beyond

For those chasing 100% completion, we provide a full breakdown of all achievements and trophies including tips for unlocking the most challenging ones.

Updates and Future Content

As *South of Midnight* continues to evolve with DLCs and updates, we'll provide insights on how to approach new content and stay ahead of the curve.

In short, this guide is designed to enhance your gaming experience, helping you not only survive the dark world of *South of Midnight* but thrive in it. Whether you're here for the story, the strategy, or simply to uncover every secret the game has to offer, this guide will ensure you walk away with a deeper understanding and maybe a few ghost stories to tell.

CHAPTER 2: SYSTEM REQUIREMENTS AND INSTALLATION

Minimum and Recommended Specifications

Before diving into the dark and mesmerizing world of *South of Midnight*, it's essential to ensure your system is ready to handle the game's rich graphics and immersive gameplay. Below are the minimum and recommended specifications needed to run the game smoothly on PC. Console players can skip this section unless they are looking to optimize performance settings.

Minimum Specifications (For Playable Performance):

These specs are designed for those who just want to get the game running. Expect lower graphics quality and moderate frame rates.

- **Operating System:** Windows 10 (64-bit)

- **Processor (CPU):** Intel Core i5-8400 @ 2.8GHz or AMD Ryzen 5 2600

- **Graphics Card (GPU):** NVIDIA GeForce GTX 1060 (6GB) or AMD Radeon RX 580 (8GB)

- **RAM:** 8GB DDR4

- **Storage:** 70GB available space (SSD preferred but not required)

- **DirectX:** Version 12

- **Resolution:** 1080p @ 30 FPS (Low to Medium Settings)

Performance Expectations:

At minimum specs, expect lower texture quality, reduced lighting effects, and occasional frame drops in high-density areas. However, the game remains fully playable.

Recommended Specifications (For Optimal Experience):

If you want to experience *South of Midnight* as the developers intended with smooth performance, high-resolution textures, and minimal frame drops these are the specs you need.

- **Operating System:** Windows 11 (64-bit)

- **Processor (CPU):** Intel Core i7-9700K @ 3.6GHz or AMD Ryzen 7 3700X

- **Graphics Card (GPU):** NVIDIA GeForce RTX 3070 (8GB) or AMD Radeon RX 6800 (16GB)

- **RAM:** 16GB DDR4

- **Storage:** 70GB SSD (Solid State Drive highly recommended)

- **DirectX:** Version 12

- **Resolution:** 1440p @ 60+ FPS (High to Ultra Settings)

Performance Expectations:

With these specs, players can enjoy high-quality textures, realistic lighting, advanced shadow rendering, and smooth gameplay even in the most demanding combat scenarios.

Ultra and 4K Gaming (For Enthusiasts):

For those aiming to push the boundaries of performance with ray tracing and 4K resolution, these specs are ideal.

- **Processor (CPU):** Intel Core i9-12900K or AMD Ryzen 9 5900X

- **Graphics Card (GPU):** NVIDIA GeForce RTX 4080 or AMD Radeon RX 7900 XTX

- **RAM:** 32GB DDR5

- **Storage:** NVMe SSD (1TB or more)

- **Resolution:** 4K @ 60+ FPS (Ultra Settings with Ray Tracing)

Console Specifications:

- **PlayStation 5:** 4K resolution, 60 FPS (Performance Mode) / 30 FPS (Quality Mode with Ray Tracing)

- **Xbox Series X|S:** 4K resolution on Series X / 1440p on Series S, 60 FPS (Performance Mode)

Ensuring your system meets or exceeds these requirements will allow you to fully immerse yourself in the eerie and beautifully crafted world of *South of Midnight.*

Installation and Setup Guide

Installing *South of Midnight* is a straightforward process, but a few steps can ensure a smooth experience with minimal issues. Whether you're playing on PC or console, follow this guide for a seamless start.

For PC (Steam/Epic Games Store):

Step 1: Purchase and Download

1. **Buy the Game:**

   o Purchase *South of Midnight* from your preferred platform (Steam, Epic Games Store, or official website).

2. **Download the Game:**

   o Once purchased, navigate to your game library and initiate the download. Ensure you have at least **70GB** of available space.

Step 2: Optimize Installation Location

- **SSD vs. HDD:**

  o If you have an SSD, install the game there for faster loading times and better performance.

- **Disk Space Check:**

  o Ensure no other large downloads are running simultaneously to prevent slow installation speeds.

Step 3: Verify Game Files

Before launching the game for the first time, verify the integrity of the game files to avoid crashes or missing content.

- **On Steam:**

  1. Right-click on *South of Midnight* in your Library.

2. Select **Properties > Local Files > Verify Integrity of Game Files**.

- **On Epic Games Store:**

  1. Navigate to the game in your Library.

  2. Click the three-dot menu and select **Verify**.

For Console (PlayStation 5 / Xbox Series X|S):

Step 1: Purchase and Download

1. Go to the **PlayStation Store** or **Microsoft Store**.

2. Purchase *South of Midnight* and initiate the download.

3. Ensure you have enough storage space consoles require at least **70GB** of free space.

Step 2: Update the Game

Consoles automatically download patches, but it's always good to double-check.

- Go to the game on your dashboard, press **Options**, and select **Check for Updates**.

Step 3: Adjust Game Settings (Performance vs. Quality Mode)

Console players can often choose between **Performance Mode** (higher frame rates) and **Quality Mode** (better graphics).

- **Performance Mode:** 60 FPS, ideal for fast-paced gameplay.

- **Quality Mode:** 30 FPS with ray tracing and enhanced visuals.

Additional Tips for a Smooth Setup

1. Disable Background Apps (PC)

- Close apps like Discord, Chrome, and other background processes to free up system resources.

2. Update Your Drivers (PC)

- Ensure your GPU drivers are up to date.

    o **NVIDIA:** Download the latest drivers via **GeForce Experience**.

    o **AMD:** Update through **AMD Radeon Software**.

3. Enable Cloud Saves

- Enable cloud saves on Steam/Epic Games or consoles to avoid losing progress.

4. Check for Day-One Patches

- Many modern games receive critical day-one updates. Always install the latest patches before starting the game.

By following these steps, you can avoid most technical issues and start your journey through the eerie, atmospheric world of *South of Midnight* without interruption. Let the haunting adventure begin!

First-Time Configuration and Settings

Once *South of Midnight* is installed, optimizing your settings for the best experience is crucial. Whether you're prioritizing performance, immersion, or accessibility, configuring the game properly will enhance your journey through its eerie world.

Initial Setup

1. Launching the Game for the First Time

- On **PC**, open the game via Steam, Epic Games, or your chosen platform.

- On **consoles**, select *South of Midnight* from your game library.

- The first time you start the game, you may be prompted to download additional updates or patchesallow this to complete for the best experience.

Graphics and Performance Settings (PC)

These settings help balance performance and visual quality depending on your system's capability.

Recommended Settings Based on Hardware

Setting	Low-End PCs (Min Spec)	Mid-Range PCs (Rec. Spec)	High-End PCs (4K & Ultra)
Resolution	1080p	1440p	4K
Graphics Preset	Medium	High	Ultra
Anti-Aliasing	FXAA	TAA	DLSS/FSR (if supported)
Shadows	Low	High	Ultra
Texture Quality	Medium	High	Ultra
Ray Tracing	Off	Medium	High/Ultra
V-Sync	On (to prevent tearing)	On (if needed)	Off (for higher FPS)

For Performance Boost:

- **Lower Shadow Quality** – Shadows can be demanding; reducing them improves FPS.

- **Disable Motion Blur & Depth of Field** – These settings add cinematic effects but can lower performance.

- **Enable DLSS (NVIDIA) or FSR (AMD)** – If supported, these options boost FPS without significant visual loss.

Display and Audio Settings

1. Display Settings (All Platforms)

- **Brightness & Contrast:** Adjust according to visibility in darker areas.

- **Field of View (FOV):** If available, setting this to **80-100** gives a wider view without too much distortion.

- **HDR (If Supported):** Enable HDR for richer colors on compatible displays.

2. Audio Settings

- **Subtitles:** Turn on for a better understanding of dialogue.

- **Sound Levels:** Adjust **Music, Dialogue, and Sound Effects** individually.

- **3D Audio (PS5 & Xbox Series X|S):** Enables directional sound for enhanced immersion.

Gameplay and Controls

1. Control Customization

- Adjust keybindings (PC) or remap controller inputs (Console).

- Sensitivity settings for aiming and movement can be adjusted based on preference.

2. Difficulty Settings

- **Story Mode:** For players who want to focus on exploration and narrative.

- **Standard:** Balanced challenge, recommended for most players.

- **Survivor:** Tougher enemies, fewer resourcesideal for veteran players.

Accessibility Settings

South of Midnight includes features for players who need additional support:

- **Colorblind Modes:** Different filters for better visibility.

- **Text-to-Speech & HUD Scaling:** Ensures readable menus.

- **Controller Assist (Console):** Helps with quick-time events and aiming.

Configuring these settings before starting your adventure ensures smooth and enjoyable gameplay, tailored to your preferences and hardware capabilities.

Troubleshooting Common Issues

Even the best games can run into technical hiccups. Below is a list of common problems in *South of Midnight* and how to fix them.

1. Game Won't Launch

Possible Causes & Fixes:

✓ PC Users:

- Ensure your system meets **minimum requirements**.

- **Verify Game Files** via Steam/Epic (Library > Right-Click Game > Properties > Verify).

- **Update Graphics Drivers** (NVIDIA/AMD).

- **Run as Administrator** (Right-click game icon > Run as Admin).

✓ Console Users:

- **Restart Your Console** (PS5/Xbox).

- **Check for Updates** (Dashboard > Options > Check for Updates).

- **Reinstall the Game** if necessary.

2. Low FPS or Lag (PC)

Fixes:

- **Lower Graphics Settings** (Shadows, Texture Quality, Effects).

- **Enable DLSS/FSR** for smoother frame rates.

- **Disable Background Apps** (Chrome, Discord, etc.).

- **Check for Overheating** (Ensure CPU/GPU temperatures are normal).

3. Audio Issues (No Sound, Crackling, Delay)

✓ **Check Audio Output:** Ensure the game is using the correct device (Settings > Sound).
✓ **Disable Background Apps:** Sometimes, Discord or other apps can interfere.
✓ **Update Audio Drivers (PC).**

4. Game Crashes or Freezes

✓ **Update Drivers & OS:** Ensure Windows and GPU drivers are up to date.
✓ **Check for Conflicting Software:** Overlays (like MSI Afterburner) can cause crashes.
✓ **Reinstall the Game** if issues persist.

5. Controller Not Working (PC)

✓ **Reconnect the Controller** (Unplug & Plug back in).
✓ **Disable Steam Input (If using Steam)**

- Go to Library > Right-click Game > Properties > Controller > Disable Steam Input.
  ✓ **Check for Firmware Updates** for your controller.

6. Multiplayer or Online Issues (If Applicable)

✓ **Check Server Status** on the official website or social media.
✓ **Restart Router & Console/PC** to refresh connection.
✓ **Use a Wired Connection** for more stable gameplay.

By following these troubleshooting steps, most issues can be resolved quickly, ensuring a smooth experience in the dark and mysterious world of *South of Midnight*. If issues persist, checking official forums or customer support can provide additional solutions.

Now that your game is configured and running smoothly, it's time to begin your adventure!

CHAPTER 3: GAMEPLAY MECHANICS

Core Controls and Interface Navigation

Mastering the controls and understanding the interface are crucial for survival in the eerie and unpredictable world of *South of Midnight*. Whether you're exploring the murky bayous, engaging in combat with shadowy creatures, or managing your inventory, fluid navigation can make or break your gameplay experience. This section will guide you through the core controls and interface layout, ensuring you're always one step ahead of the darkness.

Basic Movement and Interaction

1. Movement Controls (PC/Console)

- **Move:**

    o **PC: W, A, S, D** keys

    o **Console: Left Joystick**

- **Sprint:**

    o **PC: Shift** (Hold)

    o **Console: L3** (Press Left Joystick)

- **Jump/Climb:**

  - **PC: Spacebar**

  - **Console: X (PlayStation) / A (Xbox)**

- **Crouch/Stealth Mode:**

  - **PC: Ctrl** (Hold)

  - **Console: Circle (PS) / B (Xbox)**

2. Interaction and Exploration

- **Interact with Objects:**

  - **PC: E**

  - **Console: Square (PS) / X (Xbox)**

- **Inspect Lore Items:**

  - Examine artifacts and environmental clues to uncover the game's rich backstory.

- **Pick Up Loot:**

  - ○ Automatic when walking over smaller items; manual for weapons and larger objects.

3. Inventory and Menu Navigation

- **Open Inventory:**

  - ○ **PC: Tab**

  - ○ **Console: Touchpad (PS) / View Button (Xbox)**

- **Navigate Menus:**

  - ○ **PC:** Mouse or Arrow Keys

  - ○ **Console:** D-Pad or Left Joystick

- **Equip Items:**

  - ○ Highlight the item and press **Enter (PC)** or **X (PS) / A (Xbox)**.

- **Quick Slots:**

o   Assign weapons and consumables to quick slots for faster access during combat.

4. HUD (Heads-Up Display) Overview

The HUD in *South of Midnight* is minimalist but provides vital information:

- **Health Bar:** Top left shows your current health.

- **Stamina Bar:** Directly below health drains during sprinting and heavy attacks.

- **Minimap:** Bottom right reveals nearby points of interest and enemy locations.

- **Quest Tracker:** Top right displays current objectives.

- **Resource Counter:** Bottom left tracks ammo, crafting materials, and currency.

5. Map and Fast Travel

- **Access Map:**

  - **PC: M**

  - **Console: Options/Start Button**

- **Fast Travel Points:**

  - Discovered safe houses or landmarks can be used to travel quickly across the map.

- **Waypoints:**

  - Set custom waypoints to mark points of interest.

Mastering the Interface

Navigating *South of Midnight* efficiently means balancing exploration, inventory management, and quick decision-making. Spend time familiarizing yourself with the interface so you can focus on the game's thrilling storyline without getting bogged down by menus.

Combat System and Techniques

In *South of Midnight*, combat is more than just brute force; it's a dance of strategy, timing, and resource management. With a variety of weapons, abilities, and enemy types, understanding the nuances of combat is key to survival. Let's break down the combat mechanics and provide some essential techniques to dominate the battlefield.

1. Basic Combat Mechanics

Light and Heavy Attacks:

- **Light Attacks:**

    o **PC: Left Mouse Button**

    o **Console: R1 (PS) / RB (Xbox)**

    o Fast but deal less damage ideal for quick, agile enemies.

- **Heavy Attacks:**

    o **PC: Hold Right Mouse Button**

    o **Console: R2 (PS) / RT (Xbox)**

    o **Slower, more powerful great for staggering larger foes.**

Dodging and Blocking:

- **Dodge Roll:**

  - **PC: Spacebar + Directional Key**

  - **Console: Circle (PS) / B (Xbox)**

  - Perfect for avoiding heavy attacks or projectiles.

- **Block/Parry:**

  - **PC: Q**

  - **Console: L1 (PS) / LB (Xbox)**

  - Blocking reduces damage; parrying at the right time staggers enemies.

2. Weapons and Special Abilities

Weapon Categories:

- **Melee Weapons:**

    o **Machetes and Clubs** Best for close-quarters combat.

    o **Heavy Hammers** Deals high damage but slower swing speed.

- **Ranged Weapons:**

    o **Revolvers and Shotguns** Ideal for mid-range combat.

    o **Bows and Crossbows** Silent but deadly; perfect for stealth kills.

- **Magic Abilities (If Applicable):**

    o Special abilities tied to the game's lore. These may consume stamina or other resources.

3. Combat Techniques for Survival

1. Combos and Chain Attacks

- Combining light and heavy attacks results in devastating combos.

- **Tip:** Begin with light attacks to stagger enemies, then finish with a heavy blow.

2. Perfect Dodge and Counterattacks

- Dodging at the last second slows down time briefly, allowing for counterattacks.

- **Tip:** Practice timing to exploit enemy vulnerabilities.

3. Environmental Combat

- Use the environment to your advantage lead enemies into traps or use explosive barrels.

- **Tip:** Lure tougher enemies near ledges or explosive objects for easy kills.

4. Resource Management

- Don't waste ammo on weak enemies; save it for bosses or armored foes.

- **Tip:** Use melee weapons to conserve ammo for tougher encounters.

4. Enemy Types and Strategies

1. Grunts:

- Weak but attack in groups.

- **Strategy:** Use area-of-effect (AOE) attacks or melee weapons.

2. Armored Enemies:

- Resistant to light attacks.

- **Strategy:** Use heavy attacks or armor-piercing weapons.

3. Ranged Enemies:

- Attack from a distance.

- **Strategy:** Prioritize them first or take cover.

4. Boss Creatures:

- Unique abilities and large health pools.

- **Strategy:** Learn attack patterns, dodge frequently, and target weak points.

Pro Tips for Mastering Combat

1. **Learn Enemy Attack Patterns:**

   o Every enemy has a "tell" before attacking learning this helps in perfect dodges.

2. **Use Your Environment:**

   o Look for environmental hazards fire pits, traps, and destructible objects.

3. **Upgrade Wisely:**

   o Focus on stamina and weapon durability early on to avoid getting overwhelmed.

4. **Don't Hoard Resources:**

   o It's better to use your health potions than die with a full inventory.

Mastering the core controls and combat system will give you the edge you need to survive the nightmarish challenges that *South of Midnight* throws your way. Whether you're a cautious explorer or an aggressive fighter, adapting your playstyle to each encounter is key to thriving in this haunting world.

Exploration, Interaction, and Movement

Exploration is the heart of *South of Midnight* a dark, haunting world filled with secrets, hidden treasures, and environmental storytelling that brings its eerie setting to life. From navigating the twisted bayous to interacting with supernatural entities, understanding the nuances of movement and interaction can turn casual exploration into a rewarding and immersive experience.

1. Navigating the World

Movement Mechanics:

- **Walking and Sprinting:**

    - Walking allows you to absorb the atmosphere and avoid alerting nearby enemies.

    - Sprinting helps you cover ground quickly but drains stamina.

- **Jumping and Climbing:**

    - Some areas require precise platforming to access hidden zones.

    - Look for climbable ledges marked by subtle environmental cues, like scratches or vines.

- **Crouching and Stealth Movement:**

    - Crouching reduces noise and visibility, ideal for avoiding larger or more aggressive creatures.

2. Environmental Interaction

Looting and Collecting:

- **Collectibles:**

  - Scattered journals, letters, and relics provide lore and world-building insights.

- **Resources:**

  - Ammo, crafting materials, and health items can be found in crates, barrels, and enemy drops.

- **Locked Areas:**

  - Some doors require keys or puzzle-solving to unlock don't overlook clues hidden in the environment.

Contextual Interaction:

- **Dialogue Choices:**

  - Conversations with NPCs may offer choices that affect quests or alliances.

- **Environmental Hazards:**

  - Swamps, quicksand, or electrified surfaces can harm you.

  - **Tip:** Use these hazards against enemies when possible.

3. Exploration Rewards

Hidden Areas:

- Secret rooms or caves often house powerful weapons, unique gear, or lore pieces.

- **Tip:** Pay attention to off-the-beaten-path locations. If it looks out of place, it's worth exploring.

Side Quests and Random Events:

- The world is alive with random encounters helping a stranded NPC could yield rare items or future allies.

- Side quests often provide valuable experience points (XP) and resources.

Map Markers and Fast Travel:

- Unlock fast travel points by discovering landmarks or safe houses.

- Custom waypoints allow you to mark points of interest for later exploration.

4. Parkour and Traversal Techniques

Climbing and Vaulting:

- Leap across rooftops or vault over obstacles to escape enemies or reach vantage points.

- Parkour mechanics are fluid, rewarding players who experiment with verticality.

Zip Lines and Grappling Hooks (If Applicable):

- Some areas may feature faster traversal tools like zip lines.

- These often lead to high-tier loot or strategic combat positions.

Mastering exploration ensures you never miss a hidden chest, secret quest, or lore drop, enriching your overall experience in *South of Midnight.*

Game Modes and Progression System

To keep players engaged, *South of Midnight* offers multiple game modes and a robust progression system designed to reward exploration, combat mastery, and strategic thinking. Understanding these systems will help you tailor the experience to your playstyle while achieving steady growth in power and abilities.

1. Game Modes

Campaign Mode:

- The core story mode where you follow the main narrative, complete quests, and explore the world.

- Difficulty levels:

    o **Casual:** For players focused on story and exploration.

    o **Standard:** Balanced for challenge and immersion.

    o **Nightmare:** For hardcore players seeking brutal combat and limited resources.

Survival Mode (If Applicable):

- Focuses on endurance how long can you survive against waves of increasingly difficult enemies?

- Limited resources and permadeath may apply.

- Rewards: Unique cosmetic items or leaderboard rankings.

Multiplayer/Co-op Mode (If Applicable):

- Team up with friends or match with online players to tackle quests and bosses.

- Shared loot or individual loot systems depending on settings.

- Co-op may offer unique missions not available in single-player.

Challenge Mode (Timed or Special Events):

- Periodic in-game events with special conditions (e.g., no healing items, time limits).

- High-risk, high-reward completing these can yield rare gear or exclusive cosmetics.

2. Progression System

Progression in *South of Midnight* is built around a layered system of XP, skill trees, and equipment upgrades.

1. Experience Points (XP) and Leveling Up

- Earn XP by completing quests, defeating enemies, and discovering secrets.

- Leveling up increases core stats such as:

    - **Health:** Increases survivability.

    - **Stamina:** Extends sprinting, climbing, and heavy attack usage.

    - **Focus:** Boosts critical hit chances or magic (if applicable).

2. Skill Trees

- Divided into multiple branches such as **Combat, Survival, and Exploration**.

- Each level grants a **Skill Point**, which can be used to unlock or enhance abilities.

Sample Skill Tree Categories:

- **Combat:** Increases melee damage, attack speed, or weapon durability.

- **Survival:** Boosts health regeneration, stamina recovery, or crafting efficiency.

- **Exploration:** Unlocks better loot detection, faster traversal, or additional dialogue options.

3. Equipment Upgrades and Crafting

Crafting System:

- Collect resources to craft weapons, armor, and consumables.

- **Workbench Locations:** Found in safe houses or key locations.

Upgrade Paths:

- **Weapons:** Improve damage, range, and durability.

- **Armor:** Enhance defense and elemental resistances.

- **Consumables:** Craft powerful healing items or temporary buffs.

4. Reputation and Faction Progression (If Applicable)

- Helping certain factions or NPCs increases your reputation, unlocking special rewards.

- Faction loyalty might also affect how the story unfolds.

5. Seasonal or Endgame Content (If Applicable)

- Endgame challenges or seasonal events may offer:

    o **Exclusive loot**

    o **Limited-time quests**

    o **Leaderboard competitions**

Pro Tips for Efficient Progression:

1. **Balance Main Quests with Side Quests:**

    o Side quests often grant significant XP and gear.

2. **Upgrade Strategically:**

- Focus on stamina and resource capacity early on.

3. **Experiment with Builds:**

    - Different skill trees cater to different playstyles don't be afraid to respec.

4. **Participate in Events:**

    - Special events provide unique gear not available elsewhere.

By mastering the game modes and understanding the progression system, players can experience *South of Midnight* in a way that feels both rewarding and personal. Whether you're a casual explorer or a competitive survivor, there's always something new to discover.

CHAPTER 4: CHARACTER CLASSES AND ABILITIES

Playable Character Roles and Strengths

In *South of Midnight*, players have the opportunity to embody distinct character roles, each with unique strengths, playstyles, and abilities tailored to various combat and exploration scenarios. Whether you prefer brute force, strategic stealth, or mystical powers, understanding each role's strengths can help you dominate the battlefield and adapt to the game's challenging environments.

1. The Brawler – Strength in Close Quarters

For those who love getting up close and personal, the Brawler is the powerhouse of the game. With high health, heavy armor, and devastating melee attacks, this role thrives in close combat.

Strengths:

- **High Durability:** Can take a beating and keep fighting.

- **Powerful Melee Attacks:** Deals massive damage with hammers, clubs, or fists.

- **Knockback Abilities:** Ideal for crowd control against groups of enemies.

Weaknesses:

- **Limited Mobility:** Slower movement and dodging speed.

- **Vulnerable to Ranged Attacks:** Can be overwhelmed by snipers or magic users.

Best For:

- Players who enjoy tanking damage and overpowering enemies.

- Ideal for boss fights where sustained damage is essential.

2. The Ranger – Precision and Versatility

The Ranger excels at long-range combat, using bows, crossbows, and firearms to pick off enemies before they get too close. With moderate health but high agility, this role is perfect for players who prefer hit-and-run tactics.

Strengths:

- **Long-Range Precision:** Deals critical damage from a distance.

- **Agility and Speed:** Quick movement allows for easy repositioning.

- **Stealth Capabilities:** Can silently take down enemies without alerting others.

Weaknesses:

- **Low Health:** Vulnerable to heavy attacks.

- **Resource-Dependent:** Requires a steady supply of ammo or arrows.

Best For:

- Players who enjoy sniping or avoiding direct confrontation.

- Ideal for exploring areas with high enemy density.

3. The Mystic – Mastery of Supernatural Powers

The Mystic wields supernatural abilities tied to the game's rich lore. By channeling magic or spiritual energy, this role excels at crowd control, buffs, and elemental attacks.

Strengths:

- **Versatile Abilities:** Can heal, shield, or deal elemental damage.

- **Area of Effect (AoE) Attacks:** Ideal for managing groups of enemies.

- **Debuffs and Status Effects:** Weaken enemies or slow their movements.

Weaknesses:

- **Mana/Stamina Dependent:** Requires resource management.

- **Fragile Health:** Can be easily overwhelmed if surrounded.

Best For:

- Players who enjoy a support role or tactical combat.

- Perfect for co-op gameplay or crowd-heavy encounters.

4. The Rogue – Stealth and Evasion

The Rogue is the game's stealth specialist, emphasizing speed, agility, and critical strikes. With minimal armor but unmatched evasion, this role excels at infiltrating enemy camps and escaping unscathed.

Strengths:

- **High Evasion:** Hard to hit due to superior dodging mechanics.

- **Critical Damage:** Deals extra damage when attacking from stealth.

- **Trap Utilization:** Can set traps or use the environment against enemies.

Weaknesses:

- **Low Defense:** Vulnerable if caught in the open.

- **Requires Patience:** Not ideal for aggressive playstyles.

Best For:

- Players who enjoy stealth, sabotage, and precision kills.

- Ideal for exploration and uncovering secrets.

Choosing the Right Role for You

No single role is the "best" each caters to different playstyles. Whether you prefer tanking damage as a Brawler or picking off enemies as a Ranger, understanding your strengths and adapting to the environment will make *South of Midnight* an unforgettable experience.

Unlocking and Upgrading Abilities

As you journey through *South of Midnight*, the progression of your character hinges on unlocking and upgrading abilities that enhance combat, exploration, and survival. Whether it's improving your melee power, honing stealth skills, or mastering supernatural powers, the upgrade system allows players to tailor their character to fit their preferred playstyle.

1. How to Unlock Abilities

Experience Points (XP) System:

- Earn XP by completing main quests, side missions, defeating enemies, and discovering lore items.

- Each level gained grants **Skill Points**, which can be invested in new abilities.

Quest-Specific Rewards:

- Certain powerful abilities are locked behind major story missions or side quests.

- Special NPCs may offer unique skills unavailable through the standard skill tree.

Collectibles and Relics:

- Rare artifacts found in hidden areas can unlock passive abilities or buffs.

- **Tip:** Explore every corner these items can give you an edge in combat.

2. Skill Trees and Specializations

The skill tree in *South of Midnight* is divided into categories, allowing you to focus on specific aspects of gameplay.

1. Combat Skills:

- **Strength Boost:** Increases melee damage and attack speed.

- **Weapon Mastery:** Improves handling and reload speed of ranged weapons.

- **Stamina Surge:** Extends stamina duration for dodging and sprinting.

2. Survival and Utility Skills:

- **Health Regen:** Gradually restores health over time outside of combat.

- **Resource Efficiency:** Reduces the materials required for crafting.

- **Stealth Expertise:** Increases crouch speed and reduces noise when moving.

3. Mystic Abilities (If Applicable):

- **Elemental Attacks:** Fire, ice, or shock damage to stagger enemies.

- **Healing and Shields:** Create protective barriers or heal allies.

- **Crowd Control:** Slow or paralyze groups of enemies for easier combat.

3. Upgrade System – How It Works

Skill Points:

- Earned through leveling up or by completing specific achievements.

- Each upgrade increases power, efficiency, or duration.

Ability Tiers:

- **Tier 1:** Basic abilities with minimal resource consumption.

- **Tier 2:** Adds secondary effects, such as burn or stun.

- **Tier 3:** Maximum power with reduced cooldowns or increased range.

4. Crafting and Enhancing Abilities

Resource Requirements:

- Upgrades may require specific resources found in the game world.

- Example: **Bone Shards** for melee upgrades or **Ether Crystals** for mystic powers.

Crafting Stations:

- Visit crafting benches or NPCs who specialize in enhancements.

- Upgrade materials can be gathered from defeated enemies or bought from merchants.

5. Tips for Efficient Progression:

1. **Balance Offense and Defense:**

   o Prioritize survivability in early levels a dead character can't deal damage.

2. **Experiment with Builds:**

o   Don't hesitate to respec skill points if a build doesn't suit your playstyle.

3. **Invest in Passive Abilities:**

o   Upgrades that improve stamina, health, or resource collection pay off long-term.

4. **Keep an Eye on Cooldowns:**

o   Abilities with shorter cooldowns often provide better sustained performance.

Unlocking and upgrading abilities is about more than raw power; it's about adapting to challenges and experimenting with different builds to find what works best. Whether you're a defensive tank or an agile rogue, *South of Midnight* offers a wealth of customization to keep every playthrough fresh and rewarding.

Best Builds for Different Playstyles

In *South of Midnight*, versatility is key. Whether you prefer overwhelming enemies with brute force, striking from the shadows, or wielding supernatural powers, crafting the right build can elevate your gameplay experience. This section explores optimized builds tailored to different playstyles, helping players maximize their strengths while minimizing weaknesses.

1. The Juggernaut – Tank Build

For players who love to stand toe-to-toe with enemies, this build emphasizes survivability and raw power. With high health, damage resistance, and knockback abilities, the Juggernaut thrives in chaotic combat.

Key Skills:

- **Unbreakable Armor:** Reduces incoming damage by 30%.

- **Stamina Surge:** Increases stamina regeneration for sustained heavy attacks.

- **Ground Pound:** AoE attack that knocks back surrounding enemies.

Recommended Gear:

- **Weapons:** Heavy hammers or clubs with stagger effects.

- **Armor:** Prioritize health regen and damage reduction.

- **Consumables:** Health potions and shield boosts.

Best For:

- Fighting bosses or large groups of enemies.

- Players who prioritize durability over speed.

2. The Phantom – Stealth Assassin Build

The Phantom is ideal for players who prefer agility and precision. By emphasizing stealth, critical hits, and trap usage, this build is perfect for taking down enemies before they realize you're there.

Key Skills:

- **Silent Steps:** Increases stealth movement speed by 20%.

- **Assassin's Touch:** Critical hits from stealth deal double damage.

- **Shadow Veil:** Temporary invisibility for quick escapes.

Recommended Gear:

- **Weapons:** Dual daggers or silenced ranged weapons.

- **Armor:** Light armor with noise reduction and dodge bonuses.

- **Consumables:** Smoke bombs and stamina boosts.

Best For:

- Infiltrating enemy camps and assassinating high-priority targets.

- Players who enjoy methodical, strategic gameplay.

3. The Arcane Warden – Magic and Crowd Control Build

For those drawn to supernatural powers, this build focuses on spells, buffs, and AoE attacks. With high mana and cooldown reduction, the Arcane Warden excels at controlling the battlefield.

Key Skills:

- **Ethereal Surge:** Deals elemental damage (fire, ice, or shock) to multiple enemies.

- **Arcane Shield:** Absorbs damage and reflects a portion back to attackers.

- **Binding Roots:** Traps enemies in place, leaving them vulnerable.

Recommended Gear:

- **Weapons:** Staffs or enchanted blades with elemental damage.

- **Armor:** Robes or light armor with mana regeneration.

- **Consumables:** Mana potions and cooldown reducers.

Best For:

- Crowd control and team support in co-op play.

- Players who enjoy strategic spellcasting.

4. The Gunslinger – Ranged DPS Build

This build prioritizes ranged weapons, critical hits, and rapid fire. The Gunslinger excels in taking down enemies from a distance, maintaining mobility while dealing consistent damage.

Key Skills:

- **Quick Draw:** Increases weapon reload speed and fire rate.

- **Deadeye:** Critical hits restore a small amount of health.

- **Ricochet Shot:** Bullets bounce between nearby enemies.

Recommended Gear:

- **Weapons:** Pistols or rifles with high critical hit chances.

- **Armor:** Medium armor with movement speed boosts.

- **Consumables:** Ammo packs and damage boosters.

Best For:

- Long-range combat in open areas.

- Players who prefer high DPS with minimal risk.

5. The Hybrid – Versatile Build

If you struggle to choose between brute strength, stealth, or magic, the Hybrid offers a balanced approach. This build sacrifices specialization for flexibility, allowing you to adapt to any situation.

Key Skills:

- **Balanced Stance:** Increases health and mana slightly.

- **Versatile Combat:** Allows quick switching between melee and ranged weapons.

- **Adaptive Reflexes:** Temporarily boosts either speed or strength based on the enemy type.

Recommended Gear:

- **Weapons:** A mix of melee and ranged weapons.

- **Armor:** Medium armor with balanced stats.

- **Consumables:** Health and mana potions.

Best For:

- Players who enjoy experimenting with different playstyles.

- Those tackling diverse mission types.

Leveling Up and Skill Progression

The leveling and progression system in *South of Midnight* is designed to reward exploration, combat mastery, and strategic decision-making. Whether you're investing in powerful attacks, passive buffs, or resource management, understanding how to efficiently level up can greatly enhance your gameplay experience.

1. How the Leveling System Works

Experience Points (XP):

- Earn XP by completing:

- o **Main Quests:** Provide the highest XP rewards.

- o **Side Quests:** Often offer XP along with gear or lore items.

- o **Combat:** Defeating enemies yields smaller but consistent XP gains.

- o **Exploration:** Discovering new locations or hidden areas grants bonus XP.

2. Skill Point Allocation

With each level gained, you earn **Skill Points** to invest in various abilities. Allocating points strategically can make or break your character build.

Skill Categories:

- **Combat:** Increases weapon damage, attack speed, and critical hit rate.

- **Defense:** Boosts health, armor, and damage resistance.

- **Stamina:** Extends sprinting, dodging, and heavy attack duration.

- **Utility:** Improves crafting efficiency, resource gathering, and dialogue options.

Tips for Allocation:

- **Early Game:** Prioritize stamina and health for survivability.
- **Mid to Late Game:** Shift focus to damage output and cooldown reductions.

3. Unlocking Perks and Abilities

Certain abilities can only be unlocked by completing specific missions or reaching a level threshold.

Quest-Locked Abilities:

- Some of the most powerful abilities require progressing through the main storyline or completing faction missions.

- Example: **"Death's Embrace"** may only be unlocked after defeating a major boss.

Faction or Reputation-Based Skills:

- Helping factions or key NPCs may unlock unique perks.

- **Tip:** Balancing reputation with multiple factions offers more rewards.

4. Progression Milestones

Every 5 Levels:

- Unlock a "Milestone Ability" a powerful skill that significantly enhances combat or exploration.

- Example: **Level 10:** Unlocks double dodge rolls or a second weapon slot.

Prestige Levels (If Applicable):

- After reaching the level cap, players may prestige to gain special cosmetic items or additional skill points.

- Keeps gameplay rewarding even after the main story is complete.

5. Best Practices for Efficient Progression

1. **Complete Side Quests:** They often yield more XP per minute than grinding enemies.

2. **Explore Thoroughly:** Hidden areas with lore and collectibles offer valuable bonuses.

3. **Diversify Skill Points:** A well-rounded build is more adaptable to different missions.

4. **Save for Milestone Skills:** Some powerful abilities require multiple skill points.

Efficient leveling ensures you are always one step ahead of your enemies. With a well-thought-out skill progression plan, you can adapt to any challenge *South of Midnight* throws your way.

CHAPTER 5: WEAPONS, EQUIPMENT, AND ITEMS

Weapon Categories and Damage Types

In *South of Midnight*, survival hinges on how well you equip yourself for the battles ahead. With an extensive arsenal of weapons and varying damage types, understanding the strengths and weaknesses of each weapon category is essential. Whether you're slicing through hordes with a sword, sniping from afar, or channeling supernatural energy, this guide provides insight into every weapon type to help you choose the perfect tool for every situation.

1. Melee Weapons

Melee weapons are ideal for close-quarters combat, providing high damage output with minimal resource consumption. They are categorized by speed, range, and knockback capabilities.

Types of Melee Weapons:

- **Swords:** Balanced weapons offering moderate speed and damage.

- **Axes:** High-damage weapons with slow swing speeds, ideal for armor penetration.

- **Hammers:** Heavy weapons specializing in knockback and crowd control.

- **Daggers:** Fast but low-damage weapons with high critical hit chances.

Damage Types:

- **Slash Damage:** Effective against lightly armored enemies.

- **Blunt Damage:** Ideal for breaking armor and staggering foes.

- **Piercing Damage:** Good for precise strikes against weak points.

2. Ranged Weapons

Ranged weapons allow players to maintain a safe distance while dealing damage. With various ammunition types and firing modes, they are essential for players who prioritize positioning and precision.

Types of Ranged Weapons:

- **Bows:** Silent weapons with long-range accuracy; ideal for stealth.

- **Crossbows:** Slower than bows but deal more damage per shot.

  Firearms: Pistols, rifles, and shotguns offer high DPS but require ammo management.

- **Thrown Weapons:** Grenades or throwing knives that deal AoE or status effects.

Damage Types:

- **Ballistic Damage:** Effective against organic enemies.

- **Explosive Damage:** Great for crowd control and destroying barriers.

- **Elemental Damage:** Applies burn, freeze, or shock effects depending on the ammo type.

3. Magic and Elemental Weapons

For players who prefer supernatural combat, magic weapons provide a unique way to damage enemies and manipulate the battlefield. These weapons often scale with mana or magic stats.

Types of Magic Weapons:

- **Staffs:** Long-range weapons channeling elemental projectiles.

- **Wands:** Quick-casting weapons ideal for single-target damage.

- **Runes:** Summon traps or totems that deal ongoing damage.

- **Channeled Weapons:** Require constant mana drain but deal sustained damage.

Damage Types:

- **Fire Damage:** Causes burn-over-time effects, effective against fleshy enemies.

- **Ice Damage:** Slows or freezes enemies, reducing their movement speed.

- **Shock Damage:** Staggers mechanical or armored enemies.

- **Dark Energy:** Deals damage over time and may apply debuffs.

4. Hybrid and Unique Weapons

Hybrid weapons combine two combat styles or provide special mechanics that offer versatility in battle.

Types of Hybrid Weapons:

- **Gunblades:** Combine melee and ranged damage, ideal for flexible combat.

- **Elemental Blades:** Melee weapons with elemental properties.

- **Boomerangs:** Return to the player, offering a reusable ranged option.

- **Summoned Weapons:** Materialize briefly for powerful single-use attacks.

Damage Types:

- **Physical + Elemental:** Deals both melee and elemental damage simultaneously.

- **Status Effects:** Applies poison, bleed, or paralysis for extended damage.

Weapon Rarity and Quality

In *South of Midnight*, weapons come in various rarities that determine their power and stat bonuses.

Rarity Levels:

- **Common (Gray):** Basic weapons with minimal stats.

- **Uncommon (Green):** Slightly better stats with minor perks.

- **Rare (Blue):** Improved damage and unique passive abilities.

- **Epic (Purple):** High-end weapons with multiple perks.

- **Legendary (Gold):** Extremely powerful with game-changing abilities.

Weapon Mods:

- Attachments such as scopes, silencers, or elemental modifiers can further enhance performance.

- Example: Adding a shock mod to a rifle can temporarily disable mechanical enemies.

Choosing the Right Weapon

Consider the Situation:

- **Melee for tight spaces.**

- **Ranged for open fields or flying enemies.**

- **Magic for crowd control or specialized enemies.**

Experiment with Loadouts:

- Swapping weapons depending on the mission can maximize efficiency.

- Keep a balanced loadout with one ranged and one melee weapon for versatility.

Equip yourself wisely in *South of Midnight*, the right weapon can be the difference between life and death.

Armor and Defensive Gear

Surviving the harsh world of *South of Midnight* requires more than powerful weapons. Defensive gear such as armor, shields, and accessories provides vital protection against enemy attacks, elemental hazards, and environmental dangers. Whether you're tanking damage or dodging blows, choosing the right defensive gear is essential for any build.

1. Types of Armor

Armor is categorized by weight and protection level, each offering trade-offs between mobility and defense.

1. Light Armor

- **Pros:**

  - High mobility and faster dodge roll recovery.

  - Increases stamina and stealth effectiveness.

- **Cons:**

  - Low damage resistance.

o   Vulnerable to heavy attacks.

2. Medium Armor

- **Pros:**

    o   Balanced defense and mobility.

    o   Good for versatile playstyles.

- **Cons:**

    o   Average resistance to elemental damage.

    o   Moderately slows dodge recovery.

3. Heavy Armor

- **Pros:**

    o   Highest defense against physical and elemental damage.

    o   Best for tank builds.

- **Cons:**

  - Severely reduces movement speed.

  - Consumes more stamina when dodging.

2. Shields and Barriers

Shields and magical barriers can absorb or deflect damage, giving players time to recover or reposition during combat.

Shield Types:

- **Physical Shields:** Block melee and ranged damage but degrade over time.

- **Energy Shields:** Recharge over time but offer less durability.

- **Mystic Barriers:** Reflect a portion of the damage back to attackers.

3. Accessories and Defensive Mods

Accessories such as rings, amulets, and mods enhance defense and provide passive buffs.

Examples:

- **Ring of Resilience:** Reduces stagger duration by 30%.

- **Amulet of Vitality:** Boosts maximum health by 20%.

- **Elemental Ward Mod:** Reduces elemental damage by 15%.

4. Crafting and Upgrading Gear

In *South of Midnight*, crafting is essential for keeping your armor competitive against stronger enemies.

Resources Required:

- **Iron and Steel:** Upgrade physical armor.

- **Crystals and Ether Shards:** Enhance shields and mystical barriers.

- **Leather and Cloth:** Improve light armor mobility stats.

Upgrade Tiers:

- **Tier 1-2:** Increases base stats with minimal resource use.

- **Tier 3-4:** Adds unique perks like health regen or damage reflection.

- **Tier 5:** Maximizes stats and unlocks cosmetic customization.

Balancing Defense and Offense

The best defense is not just high armor stats it's adaptability. Balancing armor weight, shield efficiency, and accessory buffs can create a well-rounded build that survives the toughest encounters.

- **Tank players:** Prioritize heavy armor and health regeneration.

- **Stealth players:** Opt for light armor with dodge bonuses.

- **Balanced builds:** Use medium armor with cooldown reduction mods.

Survival isn't about avoiding damage it's about managing it. In *South of Midnight*, the right defensive gear can turn a challenging fight into a victorious one.

Crafting and Upgrading Equipment

In *South of Midnight*, raw power alone won't carry you through the toughest battles well-crafted and upgraded equipment will. Crafting allows players to create weapons, armor, and accessories tailored to their playstyle, while upgrading ensures these items remain effective as the game progresses. Mastering the art of crafting and upgrading not only improves combat effectiveness but also adds a strategic layer to survival and exploration.

1. Crafting Basics

Gathering Resources:

To craft or upgrade equipment, players must collect a variety of materials scattered throughout the game world. These materials are often found by:

- **Looting fallen enemies** Bosses drop rare components.

- **Exploring hidden locations** Mines, caves, and abandoned settlements yield metals and rare ores.

- **Harvesting plants and minerals** Elemental resources such as **Ether Shards** or **Flame Petals** enhance magical gear.

- **Dismantling old gear** Breaking down outdated equipment returns valuable materials.

2. Crafting Stations

Crafting is only possible at designated stations found in safe zones or player hubs. Each station specializes in a specific type of gear.

Types of Crafting Stations:

- **Blacksmith Forge:** For creating and upgrading weapons and heavy armor.

- **Tinker's Workshop:** For crafting traps, ammunition, and utility gear.

- **Arcane Altar:** For infusing weapons with elemental properties or crafting magic-based items.

- **Leatherworking Bench:** For crafting light armor and stealth accessories.

3. Upgrade Mechanics

Upgrading equipment improves its stats, unlocks new abilities, and increases its rarity level. Upgrades require both resources and in-game currency.

Upgrade Tiers:

- **Tier 1-2 (Basic):** Minimal material cost, modest stat boosts.

- **Tier 3-4 (Enhanced):** Adds passive bonuses (e.g., damage reflection, stamina regen).

- **Tier 5 (Masterwork):** Grants unique effects such as lifesteal or elemental explosions.

Example:

- **Basic Sword (Tier 1):** 50 damage, no bonuses.

- **Enhanced Sword (Tier 3):** 80 damage, 10% critical hit rate.

- **Masterwork Sword (Tier 5):** 120 damage, 20% critical rate, lifesteal on hit.

4. Special Materials and Rarity Unlocks

Certain upgrades require rare, high-value materials found only in specific regions or from high-level enemies.

Rare Materials:

- **Voidsteel:** Required for legendary weapon upgrades.

- **Obsidian Shards:** Essential for elemental resistance gear.

- **Moonstone Dust:** Increases mana efficiency on magical items.

How to Obtain Rare Materials:

- **World Events:** Participate in time-limited challenges.

- **Boss Fights:** Defeat elite enemies for high-tier loot.

- **Exploration:** Find hidden caches in remote or hard-to-reach areas.

5. Crafting Tips for Efficiency

- **Focus on Versatility:** Don't over-invest in a single weapon early on.

- **Balance Stats:** Prioritize survivability and stamina upgrades before raw damage.

- **Dismantle Wisely:** Break down old gear to reclaim rare materials.

- **Upgrade Over Crafting New:** Sometimes upgrading a favorite weapon is more resource-efficient than crafting a new one.

Crafting in *South of Midnight* is more than a feature it's a lifeline. Mastering it can turn you from prey to predator in even the harshest environments.

Best Gear Combinations for Success

No single piece of equipment can carry you through the challenges of *South of Midnight*. The key to success lies in smartly combining weapons, armor, and accessories that synergize with your playstyle.

Whether you prefer brute force, stealth, or magic, this section explores optimal gear setups to dominate the battlefield.

1. The Unstoppable Tank

Best For: Players who want to withstand overwhelming damage while dishing it back.

Recommended Setup:

- **Weapon:**

  - **Earthbreaker Maul** (Blunt damage with knockback)

- **Armor:**

  - **Titan's Bulwark** (Heavy armor with 25% damage resistance)

- **Shield:**

  - **Ironclad Barrier** (Reflects 10% of damage back to attackers)

- **Accessories:**

  - **Ring of Fortitude** (Increases health by 20%)

- Amulet of Stone Resolve (Reduces stagger duration)

Why It Works:

This build thrives on sustainability. With high health and defensive stats, you can afford to trade blows while steadily wearing down enemies.

2. The Precision Assassin

Best For: Players who excel at stealth and high-damage burst attacks.

Recommended Setup:

- **Weapon:**

  - **Shadowfang Daggers** (High critical hit rate from behind)

- **Armor:**

  - **Wraithhide Suit** (Noise reduction and faster dodge recovery)

- **Shield/Utility:**

  - **Smoke Bomb** (Creates cover for stealth repositioning)

- **Accessories:**

  - Ring of the Silent Step (Increases stealth speed)

  - Pendant of Lethality (Boosts backstab damage by 30%)

Why It Works:

This gear combination allows for quick infiltration and high-damage takedowns before enemies can retaliate.

3. The Elemental Overlord

Best For: Players who love controlling the battlefield with elemental attacks.

Recommended Setup:

- **Weapon:**

  - Stormcaller Staff (Chain lightning attacks)

- **Armor:**

  - Robes of the Ardent Flame (Boosts fire and lightning damage)

- **Shield/Utility:**

  - o **Elemental Ward** (Reduces incoming elemental damage)

- **Accessories:**

  - o **Ring of Arcane Power** (Increases spell power by 20%)

  - o **Talisman of Energy Flow** (Reduces cooldowns by 15%)

Why It Works:

This build excels in crowd control, ideal for fighting multiple enemies or slowing down fast attackers.

4. The Versatile Explorer

Best For: Players who want flexibility in combat and exploration.

Recommended Setup:

- **Weapon:**

  - o **Gunblade of the Lost** (Switches between ranged and melee damage)

- **Armor:**

    - o **Ranger's Vestments** (Medium armor with stamina regen)

- **Shield/Utility:**

    - o **Kinetic Shield** (Absorbs damage and converts it to stamina)

- **Accessories:**

    - o **Ring of the Wanderer** (Boosts movement speed by 15%)

    - o **Amulet of Resourcefulness** (Increases resource drop rate)

Why It Works:

This gear combination is ideal for players who explore frequently, allowing them to adapt to changing scenarios.

5. Endgame Legendary Setup

Best For: Players who have completed most of the game and seek maximum power.

Recommended Setup:

- **Weapon:**

  - **Voidfang Scythe** (Life drain with AoE damage)

- **Armor:**

  - **Aetherlord's Mantle** (Boosts all elemental resistances by 30%)

- **Shield/Utility:**

  - **Eclipse Barrier** (Reflects damage and grants temporary invincibility)

- **Accessories:**

  - **Ring of Infinity** (Halves cooldown times)

  - **Pendant of the Vanquished** (Boosts damage by 25% when health is below 50%)

Why It Works:

This endgame build offers unparalleled power and survivability, ideal for boss fights and high-difficulty challenges.

Combining the right gear is more than just matching stats it's about creating synergy that fits your playstyle. Whether you aim to overpower, outmaneuver, or outthink your enemies, mastering gear combinations in *South of Midnight* ensures that every battle is fought on your terms.

CHAPTER 6: STRATEGIES AND TIPS FOR SUCCESS

Beginner's Survival Guide

Starting your journey in *South of Midnight* can be both thrilling and daunting. With a vast open world filled with hostile creatures, mysterious factions, and deep gameplay mechanics, it's essential to build a solid foundation from the get-go. This survival guide is designed to help new players navigate the early game, avoid common pitfalls, and set themselves up for long-term success.

1. Understand the Game World

The world of *South of Midnight* is a dynamic, living environment where survival isn't guaranteed. From lush swamps to eerie ghost towns, each location has its own dangers and rewards.

Key Tips:

- **Explore Early, Explore Often:**

  - Early exploration reveals safe zones, crafting materials, and fast-travel points.

- **Take Notes:**

  - Keep track of resource-rich areas and enemy spawn locations.

- **Be Wary of the Day-Night Cycle:**

  - Certain enemies become stronger at night, while others only appear during the day.

2. Master the Basics of Combat

Jumping headfirst into combat without preparation is a quick way to end up defeated. Learning the basics is crucial.

Combat Fundamentals:

- **Timing Is Everything:**

  - Learn enemy attack patterns to dodge or parry at the right moment.

- **Manage Your Stamina:**

  - Attacking, blocking, and dodging drain stamina. Avoid overcommitting.

- **Use the Environment:**

  - Explosive barrels, high ground, and cover can turn the tide of battle.

- **Healing Wisely:**

  - o Heal when you have breathing room healing items have animation delays.

3. Prioritize Early Game Goals

Setting early goals helps streamline progression.

Essential Goals:

- **Find a Reliable Weapon:**

  - o Experiment until you find a weapon that suits your playstyle.

- **Upgrade Your Gear:**

  - o Prioritize upgrading armor for survivability before investing in damage.

- **Unlock Fast Travel Points:**

  - o Makes backtracking and resource farming less time-consuming.

- **Complete Side Quests:**

o   Side quests often provide valuable resources and XP.

4. Inventory and Resource Management

Your inventory space is limited manage it wisely.

Tips for Inventory Management:

- **Prioritize Rare Materials:**

    o   Don't carry too many common resources that you can easily find again.

- **Sell or Dismantle Junk Gear:**

    o   Keep inventory slots open for high-value loot.

- **Carry Essentials:**

    o   Always have healing items, stamina potions, and ammo.

5. Building Your Character

Customization is at the heart of *South of Midnight*. Your choices in abilities, weapons, and gear define your playstyle.

Best Practices:

- **Don't Spread Yourself Too Thin:**

  - o Focus on a few core stats or abilities instead of trying to master everything.

- **Synergize Gear and Skills:**

  - o Pair abilities with equipment that enhances them.

- **Adapt to the Situation:**

  - o Have different loadouts for exploration, combat, and boss fights.

With these survival tips in hand, new players can confidently embark on their journey through *South of Midnight* and enjoy a smooth progression from novice to seasoned adventurer.

Combat Strategies for Tough Encounters

The combat system in *South of Midnight* offers depth and complexity, requiring strategy and precision to overcome powerful enemies and bosses. From understanding enemy behaviors to exploiting environmental advantages, this section provides actionable strategies to help you conquer even the most challenging battles.

1. Study Your Enemies

Every enemy has strengths, weaknesses, and attack patterns that can be exploited.

Key Tips for Enemy Analysis:

- **Observe Before Attacking:**

  - Watch enemy movement patterns to learn when they're most vulnerable.

- **Use the Best Damage Type:**

  - Blunt damage for armored foes, elemental for organic enemies.

- **Exploit Status Effects:**

  - Poison, burn, and shock can drain health or stagger enemies.

2. Positioning Is Power

Where you stand in combat often determines the outcome of the fight.

Positioning Tips:

- **Maintain High Ground:**

  - Ranged attacks deal more damage, and enemies have a harder time reaching you.

- **Use Cover:**

  - Hide behind walls or obstacles to avoid ranged enemy attacks.

- **Bait and Punish:**

  - Lure enemies into predictable attack patterns, then counter.

3. Master Advanced Combat Techniques

Basic attacks only get you so far. Incorporating advanced mechanics can turn the tide in difficult encounters.

Advanced Techniques:

- **Perfect Dodge:**

  - Dodging at the last second slows time briefly, allowing for counterattacks.

- **Parry and Riposte:**

    o Blocking at the right moment stuns enemies and opens them up for critical damage.

- **Combo Chains:**

    o Certain weapon types deal increased damage when used in consecutive strikes.

- **Staggering Bosses:**

    o Consistent heavy attacks stagger bosses, interrupting their most dangerous moves.

---

4. Utilize Consumables and Buffs

Buffs and consumable items can make or break a fight, especially against tough enemies.

Essential Consumables:

- **Healing Tonics:**

    o Restore health over time, allowing you to stay in the fight longer.

- **Stamina Boosters:**

  - Increase stamina regeneration for more frequent dodging or attacking.

- **Elemental Oils:**

  - Temporarily add fire, frost, or shock damage to weapons.

- **Resistance Potions:**

  - Reduce incoming elemental damage.

5. Strategy for Boss Fights

Boss battles in *South of Midnight* are often multi-phase encounters that require patience and adaptability.

Surviving Boss Battles:

- **Phase 1 Observation:**

  - Focus on defense to learn attack patterns.

- **Phase 2 Aggression:**

- o Once you recognize safe openings, go on the offensive.

- **Phase 3 Adaptation:**

  - o Late phases often introduce new attacks stay alert.

- **Use Summons or Allies:**

  - o Certain fights allow you to summon NPC allies for assistance.

6. Overcoming Difficult Mobs

Sometimes it's not the boss that defeats you it's the mobs.

Tips for Mob Management:

- **Divide and Conquer:**

  - o Lure small groups away from the main horde.

- **Prioritize High-Damage Enemies:**

  - o Eliminate glass cannon enemies (like archers or mages) first.

- **Use AoE Attacks:**

    - Wide-sweeping attacks or explosives can thin out crowds quickly.

7. When to Retreat

Not every fight needs to be won immediately. Knowing when to retreat can save valuable resources.

When to Fall Back:

- **Low on Healing Supplies:**

    - Running out of potions in a long fight is a death sentence.

- **Underleveled Gear:**

    - If enemies are significantly higher level, come back later.

- **Out of Stamina:**

    - Running out of stamina leaves you vulnerable to devastating attacks.

Mastering combat in *South of Midnight* is a journey of trial, error, and eventual triumph. By combining patience with strategy, even the toughest encounters can become rewarding victories.

Resource Management and Optimization

In *South of Midnight*, survival isn't just about winning battles it's about managing resources wisely. Whether it's materials for crafting, currency for upgrades, or consumables for healing, efficient resource management can be the difference between thriving and barely scraping by. This section provides tips on how to gather, allocate, and optimize resources to maximize your effectiveness throughout the game.

1. Prioritize Valuable Resources

Not all resources are created equal. Some are abundant, while others are rare and essential for high-level crafting or upgrading.

Key Resource Categories:

- **Crafting Materials:** Used to create and upgrade gear.

- **Currency (Midnight Shards):** Needed for trading and upgrading.

- **Consumables:** Essential for healing, stamina regeneration, and buffs.

- **Quest Items:** Often one-time use, but crucial for progression.

Best Practices:

- **Farm Smart:**

    - Focus on high-yield farming zones where rare materials frequently spawn.

- **Sell, Don't Hoard:**

    - Sell excess common materials to free inventory space and earn currency.

- **Know What's Renewable:**

    - Common resources respawn; don't over-prioritize them.

2. Efficient Inventory Management

In a game where inventory space is limited, knowing what to carry and what to leave behind is critical.

Tips for Efficient Inventory Use:

- **Keep a Balanced Inventory:**

    - Aim for a 60/40 split between combat essentials (weapons, potions) and crafting materials.

- **Use Stash Systems:**

  - Offload rare items to stashes located in safe zones.

- **Regularly Dismantle Gear:**

  - Break down old weapons for materials rather than carrying them around.

- **Sort by Rarity:**

  - Keep legendary and rare items; sell or dismantle commons.

3. Currency Management

The in-game currency, **Midnight Shards**, is the backbone of trade and upgrades. Mismanaging this resource can slow down progression.

How to Optimize Currency Use:

- **Don't Rush Upgrades:**

  - Early-game gear quickly becomes obsolete save currency for mid to late-game equipment.

- **Invest in Durability:**

    - Focus on upgrading armor and shields before weapons to enhance survivability.

- **Complete Side Quests:**

    - Side quests often reward substantial amounts of currency.

- **Trade Smart:**

    - Some merchants sell the same item for less always compare prices.

4. Time-Efficient Farming

Spending hours farming resources can be tedious. Efficient farming methods save time and maintain the gameplay flow.

Best Farming Practices:

- **Farm During Side Quests:**

    - Combine farming with quests to maximize efficiency.

- **Target World Events:**

- o Limited-time events often yield rare materials and high currency payouts.

- **Exploit Enemy Weaknesses:**

  - o Some enemies drop rare materials when killed with specific damage types.

- **Use Resource Maps:**

  - o Mark resource-rich areas for quick return visits.

5. The Art of Optimization

Efficient resource management isn't about hoarding; it's about timing. Knowing when to spend, when to upgrade, and when to sell can significantly enhance gameplay.

Optimization Strategy:

- **Early Game:**

  - o Focus on gathering and selling low-tier resources for quick currency.

- **Mid-Game:**

  - o Prioritize upgrading gear that matches your preferred playstyle.

- **Endgame:**

    o   Invest heavily in legendary gear and unique items.

Mastering resource management ensures that you're always prepared for the challenges ahead, allowing you to focus on enjoying the game rather than worrying about running out of supplies.

Avoiding Common Pitfalls

Even the most experienced players can fall victim to mistakes that hinder progression or make the game unnecessarily challenging. This section highlights common pitfalls in *South of Midnight* and how to avoid them, ensuring a smoother, more enjoyable gameplay experience.

1. Neglecting Defensive Stats

Many players prioritize damage output, forgetting that defense is just as important.

Why This is a Problem:

- Glass cannon builds struggle in prolonged fights or against groups.

- High-damage enemies can one-shot under-armored characters.

How to Avoid It:

- **Balance is Key:**

    o Prioritize armor and health upgrades alongside weapons.

- **Use Defensive Buffs:**

    o Potions and enchantments that boost resistance can save your life.

2. Ignoring Side Quests

Focusing solely on the main story is tempting but often leads to being under-leveled.

Why This is a Problem:

- You miss out on powerful gear and essential resources.

- Side quests often provide crucial world-building context.

How to Avoid It:

- **Complete Side Quests Early:**

- Side quests are often easier at the beginning, and rewards scale with your level.

- **Check NPCs Frequently:**

  - Some side quests are time-sensitive or triggered by other events.

3. Over-Reliance on One Playstyle

Locking into a single playstyle makes it harder to adapt to different enemy types or environments.

Why This is a Problem:

- Some bosses require range, others melee or elemental damage.

- Certain environments punish specific builds (e.g., stamina-heavy builds in swampy areas).

How to Avoid It:

- **Have Multiple Loadouts:**

  - Create different builds optimized for melee, range, and magic.

- **Switch Gear Often:**

  - Adapt your loadout to the situation rather than sticking to one setup.

4. Poor Resource Allocation

Spending resources on the wrong upgrades or unnecessary items can slow progression.

Why This is a Problem:

- Resources are finite bad investments can stall gear progression.

- Some early upgrades quickly become obsolete.

How to Avoid It:

- **Research Before Upgrading:**

  - Read item descriptions and check upgrade paths before investing.

- **Save for Mid-Game:**

  - Early-game weapons become ineffective quickly; hold resources for better gear.

5. Not Using the Environment

The environment is a crucial part of *South of Midnight*'s combat and exploration mechanics.

Why This is a Problem:

- Ignoring environmental traps or resources makes fights harder.

- Overlooking climbable structures or hidden paths limits exploration.

How to Avoid It:

- **Explore Thoroughly:**

  o Climb structures, break crates, and inspect environmental objects.

- **Use Traps to Your Advantage:**

  o Lure enemies into explosive barrels or unstable terrain.

- **Exploit Terrain in Combat:**

o High ground and choke points can turn difficult fights in your favor.

6. Rushing Through the Game

Speeding through the game often results in missing crucial mechanics, lore, and valuable items.

Why This is a Problem:

- Missing lore affects story immersion.

- Skipping mechanics tutorials can leave you unprepared for harder challenges.

How to Avoid It:

- **Take Your Time:**

    o Explore every zone thoroughly.

- **Complete Tutorials:**

    o Game mechanics introduced early on are essential later.

- **Engage with NPCs:**

    o Dialogue often contains hints or unlocks hidden side quests.

By understanding and avoiding these common pitfalls, players can experience *South of Midnight* as it was intended a challenging yet rewarding adventure full of discovery and excitement.

CHAPTER 7: WALKTHROUGH – MISSIONS AND LEVELS

Main Storyline Walkthrough

The heart of *South of Midnight* lies in its gripping main storyline, a dark yet mesmerizing tale filled with rich lore, complex characters, and challenging encounters. This walkthrough is designed to guide players through each critical chapter of the main story, ensuring they never miss essential plot points or valuable loot. Whether you're here for the narrative or the thrill of battle, this guide will help you navigate every twist and turn.

1. Chapter One: Awakening in the Bayou

You awaken in the haunting wetlands of **Midnight Hollow**, disoriented and weaponless. The eerie whispers in the wind hint at something ancient stirring beneath the surface.

Objectives:

- **Find Your Bearings:**

    o Search the nearby hut for basic gear (Starter Weapon and Healing Salve).

- **Meet the Mysterious Stranger:**

    o NPC: **Old Man Drexel** provides the first quest and essential lore about the **Midnight Curse**.

- **Combat Tutorial:**

  - Face off against **Bog Lurkers** to learn basic combat mechanics.

Key Tips:

- **Search Everything:**

  - Hidden caches contain rare crafting materials.

- **Take It Slow:**

  - Bog Lurkers are weak but deadly in groups. Learn to manage stamina early.

2. Chapter Two: The Wailing Marsh

The next leg of your journey leads you to the **Wailing Marsh**, where the dead don't stay buried.

Objectives:

- **Clear the Outpost:**

- Defeat **Marsh Wraiths** to secure a fast-travel point.

- **Solve the Puzzle of the Ancient Totems:**

  - Align the runes in the correct order to open the gate to the **Hollow Temple**.

- **Defeat the Swamp Matron (Mini-Boss):**

  - Exploit her vulnerability to **fire damage** to win the fight.

Key Tips:

- **Bring Antidotes:**

  - The swamp is full of poisonous creatures.

- **Use the Environment:**

  - Tall grass and trees can help break enemy line of sight.

3. Chapter Three: City of Lost Echoes

Entering the ruins of the once-thriving **Ivory Bastion**, players encounter the first major faction **The Pale Covenant**, a group shrouded in mysticism.

Objectives:

- **Make Peace or Go to War:**

  - Your choices here shape future encounters.

- **Infiltrate the Cathedral of Whispers:**

  - Collect three keys from faction leaders.

- **Boss Fight: The Voiceless Archbishop**

  - A powerful enemy with three phases adapt quickly to each.

Key Tips:

- **Dialogue Choices Matter:**

  - Choose your words carefully; allies or enemies are made here.

- **Use Elemental Weapons:**

    o Each boss phase is weak to a different element.

4. Chapter Four: The Broken Veil

The world begins to change as reality frays at the edges. Strange phenomena alter familiar locations.

Objectives:

- **Investigate the Rifts:**

    o Close three rifts to stabilize the region.

- **Uncover the Truth About the Veil:**

    o NPC: **Elyra, the Riftwalker**, provides essential lore.

- **Boss Encounter: The Riftborn Behemoth**

    o A challenging foe requiring mobility and patience.

Key Tips:

- **Prepare for Status Effects:**

    - The boss deals heavy **arcane damage** and inflicts **slow**.

- **Bring Backup:**

    - Summonable allies can help manage mobs during the fight.

5. Final Chapter: Midnight's End

The culmination of your journey brings you face-to-face with the true source of the Midnight Curse.

Objectives:

- **Storm the Fortress of Dread:**

    - Fight through waves of elite enemies.

- **Boss Fight: The Hollow King**

    - A two-phase fight testing every skill you've learned.

- **Make the Final Choice:**

  o Sacrifice or salvation the choice affects the ending.

Key Tips:

- **Stock Up:**

  o Healing items and stamina potions are essential.

- **Master Dodging:**

  o The boss's final phase has one-hit-kill mechanics.

Side Quests and Optional Content

While the main storyline offers a compelling narrative, *South of Midnight* is filled with rich side content that expands the lore, offers rare rewards, and provides unique gameplay experiences. Whether you're looking for powerful gear or just want to explore more of the world, side quests are well worth your time.

1. Faction Quests

The game features three major factions, each with its own questline.

Factions:

- **The Pale Covenant:**

  - Questline: "Whispers of the Lost"

  - Rewards: Unique armor set with stealth bonuses.

- **The Iron Vanguard:**

  - Questline: "Strength Through Unity"

  - Rewards: High-damage two-handed weapon.

- **Children of the Mist:**

  - Questline: "Echoes in the Fog"

  - Rewards: Arcane-based weapons and trinkets.

2. Legendary Hunts

Legendary beasts roam the lands of *South of Midnight,* offering challenging fights with high-risk, high-reward gameplay.

Notable Hunts:

- **The Swamp Wyrm:**

  - Found in **Midnight Hollow**, this beast drops rare crafting materials.

- **The Pale Stalker:**

  - A stealth-based encounter that tests patience and timing.

- **King of Cinders:**

  - Defeating this fire-based beast grants one of the best weapons in the game.

3. Hidden Lore and Collectibles

Exploration is rewarded with lore entries, journals, and hidden items that expand the game's backstory.

Types of Collectibles:

- **Ancient Tomes:**

  - Reveal the history of the Midnight Curse.

- **Lost Letters:**

    o   Provide insight into NPC motivations.

- **Totems and Runes:**

    o   Used to unlock secret areas and gear.

4. Optional Bosses

These are not required to finish the game but offer significant rewards.

Notable Optional Bosses:

- **The Shadow Queen:**

    o   Found in the **Ruins of Ebonhall**, this boss drops legendary magic gear.

- **The Hollow Knight:**

    o   An elite enemy that challenges your combat reflexes.

- **Eater of Stars:**

    o   One of the hardest bosses in the game, dropping unique cosmic-themed weapons.

5. Replay Value and Endgame Content

Once the credits roll, the journey isn't over. New Game Plus (NG+) and dynamic world events offer reasons to keep playing.

Endgame Activities:

- **New Game Plus (NG+):**

    o Enemies are tougher, but loot is better.

- **Faction Wars:**

    o Compete for dominance with shifting world states.

- **Seasonal Events:**

    o Limited-time events offer exclusive rewards.

By diving deep into the side quests and optional content, players can extend their journey through *South of Midnight*, discovering hidden stories and powerful loot while keeping the experience fresh and rewarding.

Boss Battles and How to Defeat Them

Boss battles in *South of Midnight* are more than just tests of strength they are dynamic encounters that challenge players to master combat mechanics, resource management, and quick decision-making. Each boss has unique abilities, phases, and weaknesses, making every fight a memorable experience. In this section, we'll break down key boss encounters, providing strategies to overcome even the toughest foes.

1. Swamp Matron Guardian of the Wailing Marsh

The **Swamp Matron** is the first mini-boss you'll face. Despite being an early encounter, she can overwhelm players who underestimate her.

Location:

- Wailing Marsh, near the Broken Totem.

Abilities:

- **Poison Mist:** Creates a poisonous cloud that deals damage over time.

- **Enraged Swipes:** Becomes faster and more aggressive when below 50% health.

- **Summon Bog Lurkers:** Calls minions to overwhelm players.

How to Defeat Her:

- **Exploit Elemental Weakness:**

    o She is vulnerable to **fire damage**, so use fire-coated weapons or flame spells.

- **Stay Mobile:**

  - Dodge-roll to avoid the poison mist and reposition to high ground when overwhelmed.

- **Kill the Minions First:**

  - Bog Lurkers are weak but can block your escape routes.

2. The Voiceless Archbishop Keeper of the Cathedral of Whispers

A powerful entity with a tragic backstory, the **Voiceless Archbishop** tests both patience and precision.

Location:

- Cathedral of Whispers, Ivory Bastion.

Abilities:

- **Echo Wave:** Sends out a sound-based shockwave that staggers players.

- **Summon Choir of the Lost:** Minions that amplify his attack damage.

- **Phase Two Lament of the Lost:** Releases a sustained AOE attack that drains stamina.

How to Defeat Him:

- **Bring Silence Talismans:**

  - Reduces the duration of the Echo Wave stagger effect.

- **Take Out Minions Quickly:**

  - The longer they stay alive, the stronger his attacks become.

- **Use Interrupt Skills:**

  - Heavy attacks can stagger him before he releases the Lament of the Lost.

3. The Riftborn Behemoth Manifestation of the Broken Veil

One of the most challenging mid-game bosses, the **Riftborn Behemoth** is an ethereal entity that warps reality itself.

Location:

- The Broken Veil, near the final rift.

Abilities:

- **Temporal Distortion:** Slows player movement for 5 seconds.

- **Arcane Blast:** Fires a high-damage projectile with tracking.

- **Summon Riftlings:** Minions that explode on contact.

How to Defeat It:

- **Equip Anti-Arcane Gear:**

    o Reduces incoming arcane damage by 30%.

- **Use Mobility Skills:**

    o Temporal Distortion can be mitigated with skills that grant immunity frames.

- **Attack Between Phases:**

    o The Behemoth has recovery windows after every third attack.

4. The Hollow King Final Boss

The final encounter is a two-phase battle against the **Hollow King**, the being behind the Midnight Curse. This fight tests every skill you've learned.

Location:

- Fortress of Dread, Midnight's End.

Phase One: The Tyrant's Fall:

- **Shadow Claws:** Fast melee attacks that drain stamina.

- **Void Rift:** Summons an area of darkness where healing is reduced.

Phase Two: The King Reborn:

- **Black Sun Nova:** A massive AOE attack that kills in one hit.

- **Summon Phantom Knights:** Spectral enemies that must be defeated to lower his shield.

How to Defeat Him:

- **Manage Stamina:**

    o Don't overcommit to attacks; keep stamina for dodging.

- **Use Healing Over Time Items:**

    o These bypass the Void Rift's healing debuff.

- **Attack After Nova:**

    o Black Sun Nova leaves him vulnerable for 10
      seconds.

Choices and Consequences

In *South of Midnight*, the choices you make shape the world around
you. From alliances to moral dilemmas, every decision impacts how
the story unfolds, which characters survive, and the ending you
receive. This section explores key choices and their far-reaching
consequences.

1. Aligning with a Faction

Early in the game, you are given the choice to ally with one of three
factions:

- **The Pale Covenant:** A mysterious order focused on
  maintaining the balance of power.

- **The Iron Vanguard:** A militaristic group striving for control
  over Midnight Hollow.

- **Children of the Mist:** Nomadic survivalists who prioritize
  freedom over order.

Consequences:

- **Ally Perks:**

    o Each faction grants unique gear and abilities.

- **Enemy Relations:**

  o Allying with one faction may turn another hostile.

- **Endgame Outcomes:**

  o Your chosen faction may assist or abandon you in the final battle.

2. Moral Dilemmas

Throughout the game, you'll face difficult moral choices with no clear right or wrong.

Key Decisions:

- **Saving or Sacrificing NPCs:**

  o Saving certain characters may yield short-term benefits, but they may betray you later.

- **Accepting or Rejecting Forbidden Powers:**

  o Dark powers offer immense strength but at the cost of health or reputation.

- **Betraying Allies for Personal Gain:**

  o Some choices allow you to turn on allies for legendary loot.

Consequences:

- **Character Development:**
  - NPCs remember your actions, affecting future interactions.

- **Reputation System:**

  - Good or evil actions shift how factions and townspeople treat you.

- **Ending Variations:**

  - Certain endings are only accessible with high morality or infamy.

3. Player Choice in Combat

Even in battle, choices matter. The way you approach a fight can drastically change its outcome.

Key Combat Decisions:

- **Mercy or Execution:**

  - Sparing defeated enemies may lead to future alliances.

- **Using Environmental Traps:**

  - Traps can help you win battles but may harm civilians if misused.

Consequences:

- **Loot Variation:**
  - Killing bosses offers rare loot; sparing them may yield unique abilities.

- **Narrative Impact:**
  - o Mercy is remembered allies may come to your aid later.

4. Endings Based on Choices

South of Midnight offers multiple endings based on the choices made throughout the game.

Major Ending Paths:

- **The Light of Redemption:**

  - o Achieved by consistently making selfless decisions.

- **The Path of Tyranny:**

  - o Requires ruthless and self-serving choices.

- **The Balance of Midnight:**

  - o Balancing morality leads to a neutral, bittersweet ending.

Unlocking Secret Endings:

- **Complete All Side Quests:**

  - o Some endings require saving key characters.

- **Explore Lore Areas:**

  - o Secret choices unlocked by discovering ancient tomes.

In *South of Midnight*, every choice leaves a mark. Whether you seek power, peace, or something in between, how you play determines how your story ends.

CHAPTER 8: SECRETS, COLLECTIBLES, AND EASTER EGGS

Hidden Locations and Special Items

One of the most exciting aspects of *South of Midnight* is its rich world filled with hidden locations and rare items waiting to be discovered. Exploring every corner, solving environmental puzzles, and paying attention to subtle lore hints can lead to powerful weapons, unique gear, and valuable resources. This section covers the most intriguing hidden locations and the special items they contain.

1. The Forgotten Cavern

Tucked away behind a waterfall in the **Wailing Marsh**, this cavern is easy to miss but offers rich rewards.

How to Find It:

- Look for glowing runes on the rocks near the waterfall.

- Use a **Spirit Lantern** (found during the "Echoes of the Past" quest) to reveal the entrance.

Notable Loot:

- **Moonlit Dagger:** A fast weapon with high critical damage.

- **Amulet of Whispered Echoes:** Grants increased stealth and perception.

2. The Black Market in Hollow Reach

In the city of **Ivory Bastion**, a hidden black market offers powerful items not found anywhere else.

How to Access It:

- Speak to **Merchant Krael** in the market district.

- Complete the quest **"A Favor in the Dark"** to earn his trust.

Notable Loot:

- **Phantom Cloak:** Reduces enemy detection range.

- **Shard of Midnight:** A crafting material used to upgrade legendary weapons.

3. The Ruins of Ebonhall

This haunted castle was once home to the **Order of the Veil**, a secretive faction that dabbled in forbidden magic.

How to Find It:

- Complete the quest **"Voices of the Past"** to receive the **Veilstone Key**.

- Access the ruins through the **Shattered Gate** in the **Crimson Glade**.

Notable Loot:

- **Ring of Eternal Night:** Increases stamina regeneration and critical hit chance.

- **Grimcaller's Blade:** A two-handed sword that steals health on hit.

4. The Silent Sanctum

A labyrinthine dungeon filled with traps and puzzles, the **Silent Sanctum** tests both skill and wit.

How to Find It:

- Solve the **Three Sigil Puzzle** in the **City of Lost Echoes**.

- The entrance is located beneath the city's main cathedral.

Notable Loot:

- **Eclipse Bow:** A legendary bow that deals arcane damage.

- **Tome of Forgotten Lore:** Unlocks secret dialogue with certain NPCs.

5. The Veil's Edge

At the farthest reaches of the map lies the **Veil's Edge**, a reality-warped zone where time and space are unstable.

How to Find It:

- Collect three **Void Crystals** from **Riftborn Behemoths**.

- Place the crystals on the **Altar of Echoes** in **Midnight's End**.

Notable Loot:

- **Crown of the Hollow King:** Grants immunity to status effects.

- **Heart of the Rift:** Used to craft the best armor set in the game.

Pro Tips for Finding Hidden Loot:

- **Listen to NPC Dialogue:** Many characters drop subtle hints about hidden locations.

- **Interact with the Environment:** Pushable walls, climbable ledges, and glowing symbols often lead to secrets.

- **Explore Thoroughly:** Revisiting old areas with new abilities can reveal previously inaccessible areas.

Secret Bosses and Challenges

South of Midnight is known for its challenging secret bosses, each offering unique loot and testing players in ways the main game does not. These encounters are optional but provide some of the best rewards in the game.

1. The Shadow Queen

A legendary spirit haunting the **Ruins of Ebonhall**, the **Shadow Queen** is a powerful entity known for her unpredictable attacks.

How to Find Her:

- Collect the **Three Shards of Twilight** from optional side quests.

- Place them on the altar in the throne room of **Ebonhall Keep**.

Battle Mechanics:

- **Phase One:** Teleports frequently, using shadow bolts.

- **Phase Two:** Summons mirror images to confuse players.

Rewards:

- **Queen's Shroud:** Increases stealth and movement speed.

- **Nightfang Blade:** Deals shadow damage and scales with agility.

2. The Pale Stalker

This elusive beast roams the **Crimson Glade** at night. Its battle is a test of patience and precision.

How to Find It:

- Wait until midnight in-game time and follow the howling sounds.

- Use a **Hunter's Charm** to reveal its tracks.

Battle Mechanics:

- **Ambush Attacks:** Strikes from stealth, requiring constant awareness.

- **Bleed Effect:** Causes damage over time unless treated.

Rewards:

- **Stalker's Claw:** A dagger with a high critical hit rate.

- **Ring of the Hunt:** Increases damage to bleeding enemies.

3. Eater of Stars

One of the hardest bosses in the game, the **Eater of Stars** is a cosmic entity found at the **Veil's Edge**.

How to Find It:

- Collect three **Stellar Orbs** from high-level rift enemies.

- Place them on the **Obelisk of Light** to summon the boss.

Battle Mechanics:

- **Gravity Well:** Pulls players towards the center, making movement difficult.

- **Starburst Explosion:** Massive AOE with a one-hit kill potential.

Rewards:

- **Celestial Aegis:** A shield that reflects magic damage.

- **Voidwalker's Mantle:** Reduces cooldown times for abilities.

4. The Hollow Knight

A remnant of the old order, the **Hollow Knight** is a melee powerhouse found in the **Cathedral of Whispers**.

How to Find It:

- Complete the **Order's Last Stand** questline.

- Use the **Sigil of Valor** to open the hidden crypt.

Battle Mechanics:

- **Unbreakable Guard:** Can block nearly all frontal attacks.

- **Execution Strike:** Heavy attack that deals massive damage.

Rewards:

- **Knight's Vow:** A ring that increases defense and stagger resistance.

- **Valor's Edge:** A sword that scales with strength and courage stats.

5. Trials of the Ancients

Not a single boss but a gauntlet of increasingly difficult enemies, the **Trials of the Ancients** is the ultimate test of endurance.

How to Find It:

- After completing the main story, revisit the **Broken Veil**.
- The trials are unlocked through the **Elder's Gate**.

Battle Mechanics:

- **Randomized Enemies:** Each round introduces different enemy types.

- **Environmental Hazards:** Traps and AOE zones force constant movement.

Rewards:

- **Champion's Emblem:** Increases all stats by 10%.
- **Midnight Slayer Armor:** The best endgame armor set.

Pro Tips for Secret Bosses:

- **Come Prepared:** Stock up on potions, antidotes, and crafting materials.

- **Study Patterns:** Each boss has a unique attack rhythm learn it before committing to aggressive play.

- **Don't Give Up:** These fights are designed to be hard. Keep adjusting your strategy until you succeed.

Discovering and defeating these secret bosses not only provides bragging rights but also offers the best gear and a richer understanding of *South of Midnight*'s lore.

Unlockable Content and Endings

One of the most rewarding aspects of *South of Midnight* is its vast array of unlockable content and multiple endings. From secret weapons and hidden quests to narrative-altering decisions, the game offers players the chance to experience unique outcomes based on their choices. This section explores the key unlockables and how to achieve each of the game's distinct endings.

1. Unlockable Content

Hidden Weapons and Gear

- **The Duskblade:** A legendary sword that deals bonus damage to shadow creatures.

  - **How to Unlock:** Complete the side quest **"The Last Light"** by helping **Elder Thorne** defend the **Crimson Glade**.

- **The Everflame Bow:** A powerful ranged weapon with infinite fire arrows.

  - **How to Unlock:** Defeat the secret boss **Ashborn Wyrm** in the **Molten Hollows**.

- **Armor of the Lost King:** Boosts stamina recovery and health regeneration.

  - **How to Unlock:** Collect five **Royal Sigils** scattered across the **Ivory Bastion**.

Secret Quests and Hidden Areas

- **The Whispering Woods:** A mysterious forest that changes layout every time you enter.

    - **How to Unlock:** Find the **Rune of Echoes** by completing the puzzle in the **Silent Sanctum**.

- **Trial of the Forgotten:** A series of battles against past champions.

    - **How to Unlock:** Speak to **Ghost of the First Guardian** after completing the main storyline.

Exclusive Cosmetics and Titles

- **Midnight Slayer Skin:** A cosmetic armor set with a dark, ethereal glow.

    - **How to Unlock:** Complete all boss encounters without dying.

- **Title: "The Eternal Watcher"**

    - **How to Unlock:** Collect every lore entry in the game.

2. Endings and How to Unlock Them

South of Midnight features multiple endings shaped by the choices players make throughout the game. Each ending offers a different perspective on the story, adding replay value and emotional depth.

The Light of Redemption

- **Path:** For players who make altruistic and selfless choices, prioritize saving NPCs, and avoid power-hungry decisions.

- **Key Choices:**

  - Spare the **Hollow King** in the final battle.

  - Help the **Iron Vanguard** liberate **Midnight Hollow**.

- **Outcome:**

  - The curse is lifted, and the world returns to peace. The player is celebrated as a hero.

The Path of Tyranny

- **Path:** For players who make selfish choices, prioritize power, and show little regard for alliances.

- **Key Choices:**

  - Betray the **Pale Covenant** for the **Children of the Mist**.
  - Absorb the power of the **Void Rift** instead of sealing it.

- **Outcome:**

  o The player becomes the new ruler of **Midnight Hollow**, feared by all.

The Balance of Midnight

- **Path:** For players who walk the line between good and evil, making pragmatic choices.

- **Key Choices:**

  o Help the **Pale Covenant** maintain the balance of power.

  o Spare or kill bosses based on tactical advantage.

- **Outcome:**

  o The curse is partially lifted. Peace is temporary, but the cycle continues.

The Forgotten Legacy (Secret Ending)

- **Path:** Requires collecting all **Ancient Tomes** and discovering the truth about **Midnight's Origin**.

- **Key Choices:**

  o Complete the quest **"Echoes of Eternity."**

  o Defeat the **Eater of Stars** and return its heart to the **Veil's Edge Altar**.

- **Outcome:**

  - The player becomes a guardian of time, watching over the world from beyond reality.

The Hollowed Veil (Bad Ending)

- **Path:** Triggered when the player makes consistently chaotic or destructive choices.

- **Key Choices:**

  - Betray key allies, kill innocent NPCs, and seek forbidden powers.

- **Outcome:**

  - The world is consumed by darkness, and the player is trapped in an endless loop of suffering.

Pro Tips for Unlocking All Endings:

- **Create Multiple Saves:** Keep separate save files before key decision points.

- **Experiment with Choices:** Even small actions can influence the ending you receive.

- **Replay the Game:** Each playthrough offers new dialogue and different perspectives.

Developer Easter Eggs and References

The developers of *South of Midnight* have packed the game with hidden references and playful Easter eggs that reward players for paying attention to the smallest details. These secrets range from nostalgic nods to other games to humorous interactions that break the fourth wall. Let's uncover some of the best hidden gems.

1. Homage to Classic Games

- **The Pixelated Shield:**

  - Found in the **Vault of Memories**, this low-resolution shield is a nod to classic 16-bit RPGs.

  - **Effect:** Offers minimal protection but makes enemies explode into pixels when defeated.

- **The Konami Tomb:**

  - In the **Whispering Woods**, there is a tombstone with the code **"UP, UP, DOWN, DOWN, LEFT, RIGHT, LEFT, RIGHT, B, A"** etched on it.

  - **Effect:** Entering the code grants temporary invincibility for 30 seconds.

2. Hidden Developer Messages

- **The Wall of Gratitude:**

    - In the **Cathedral of Whispers**, one of the walls has faint etchings with the names of the game developers.

    - Interacting with it triggers a voiceover saying, **"Thanks for playing you made this journey worth it."**

- **NPC Named "Chatterbox":**

    - In **Ivory Bastion**, there's an NPC who comments on how often players talk to him.

    - After 100 interactions, he breaks the fourth wall and says, **"You know, I have other players to talk to."**

3. Pop Culture References

- **The Sword in the Swamp:**

    - A sword resembling **Excalibur** is found in the **Wailing Marsh**.

    - It requires **50 Strength** to pull out, but once obtained, it deals massive damage.

- **The Ring of Power:**

  - Found in the **Molten Hollows**, this ring grants invisibility but causes the player to hear unsettling whispers.

  - A clear nod to **The Lord of the Rings**.

4. Humorous Items and Interactions

- **The Chicken of Doom:**

  - In the village of **Evershade**, attacking a chicken will summon an invincible super-chicken that chases the player for 5 minutes.

  - Defeating it (if you survive) drops the **Golden Feather**, which increases loot rarity.

- **The Mug of Infinite Ale:**

  - Found in the **Drunken Drake Tavern**, this item causes the screen to blur slightly for 10 minutes when used.

  - Consuming it five times in a row makes the player pass out and wake up in a random location.

Why These Easter Eggs Matter:

- **They Add Personality:** Easter eggs give the game charm and humor, making it memorable.

- **They Reward Exploration:** Players who take the time to explore every nook and cranny are rewarded with laughs and powerful gear.

- **They Build Community:** Players love sharing discoveries, adding to the game's lasting appeal.

So, keep your eyes peeled you never know when you might stumble upon a hidden gem in *South of Midnight*!

CHAPTER 9: ACHIEVEMENTS AND TROPHIES

Complete List of Achievements and Trophies

Achievements and trophies in *South of Midnight* are not just milestones; they tell the story of your journey through the game. Whether you're a casual gamer or a dedicated completionist, collecting these accolades offers both bragging rights and in-game rewards. Below is a categorized list of all achievements and trophies, broken down by gameplay aspects.

Storyline Achievements

1. **Midnight's Call** Complete the prologue.

2. **Echoes of the Past** Finish Chapter 1.

3. **Shattered Bonds** Witness the betrayal of a major ally.

4. **The Hollow King Falls** Defeat the Hollow King.

5. **Cycle Unbroken** Finish the main storyline with any ending.

6. **Keeper of the Veil** Unlock the **"Forgotten Legacy"** secret ending.

Exploration Achievements

1. **Cartographer's Dream** Fully uncover the entire game map.

2. **Hidden No More** Discover all hidden locations.

3. **Master of Secrets** Collect every lore book and journal.

4. **Whispered Paths** Travel through 50 secret passages.

5. **Relic Hunter** Find 20 unique relics scattered across the world.

Combat Achievements

1. **First Blood** Defeat your first enemy.

2. **Death Bringer** Defeat 1,000 enemies.

3. **Boss Breaker** Defeat every main and optional boss.

4. **Unstoppable Force** Achieve a 100-hit combo.

5. **Parry Perfection** Successfully parry 50 attacks in a row without taking damage.

Roleplay and Decision-Based Achievements

1. **Saint of the Light** Make 10 morally good choices.

2. **Master Manipulator** Make 10 morally gray or manipulative choices.

3. **Shadow of Midnight** Make 10 morally evil choices.

4. **Diplomat** Resolve 5 major conflicts through dialogue.

5. **Betrayer's End** Betray all three major factions in a single playthrough.

Crafting and Resource Management Achievements

1. **Apprentice Blacksmith** Craft your first weapon.

2. **Master of Craft** Fully upgrade a legendary weapon.

3. **Potion Master** Brew every type of potion available.

4. **Resourceful Survivor** Complete the game without running out of key resources.

5. **Eco-Friendly** Finish the game without using any health potions.

Difficulty and Skill-Based Achievements

1. **Midnight Warrior** Complete the game on **Hard** difficulty.

2. **No Room for Error** Complete the game on **Permadeath** mode.

3. **Flawless Victor** Defeat a major boss without taking any damage.

4. **Speedrunner's Edge** Complete the game in under 10 hours.

5. **Jack of All Trades** Master all character classes in a single playthrough.

Miscellaneous and Fun Achievements

1. **Chicken Whisperer** Survive the attack of the **Chicken of Doom**.

2. **Bottoms Up!** Pass out from drinking the **Mug of Infinite Ale**.

3. **Developer's Secret** Find the **Wall of Gratitude** in the **Cathedral of Whispers**.

4. **Midnight's Muse** Spend 1 hour listening to bard songs in the taverns.

5. **Fashion Icon** Collect and wear 10 unique cosmetic armor sets.

How to Unlock Difficult Achievements

Some achievements in *South of Midnight* require strategy, patience, and exceptional skill. This section provides tips and guidance to help you conquer the hardest challenges the game has to offer.

1. No Room for Error Complete the Game on Permadeath Mode

Why It's Hard:

- **Permadeath Mode** means if you die, your entire save file is deleted.

- Enemies hit harder, and healing resources are scarce.

Pro Tips:

- **Play Cautiously:** Avoid rushing into fights. Scout enemy patterns before engaging.

- **Use Ranged Combat:** Keeping your distance gives you more time to react.

- **Save Resources:** Hoard potions and high-tier gear for late-game boss fights.

- **Master Parrying:** Perfect timing can turn difficult fights into manageable ones.

2. Flawless Victor Defeat a Major Boss Without Taking Damage

Why It's Hard:

- Major bosses have complex attack patterns, environmental hazards, and high damage output.

Pro Tips:

- **Study the Boss:** Observe attack patterns and animations before attempting flawless runs.

- **Use Evasive Abilities:** Max out **Dodge** and **Parry** skills for better survivability.

- **Equip the Right Gear:** Use armor that boosts stamina and shields that absorb damage.

- **Practice with Minibosses:** Hone your timing on less challenging enemies first.

3. Speedrunner's Edge Complete the Game in Under 10 Hours

Why It's Hard:

- A typical playthrough can take 30-40 hours.
- Requires optimized routing and skipping optional content.

Pro Tips:

- **Skip Non-Essentials:** Avoid side quests unless they yield significant upgrades.

- **Memorize Maps:** Knowing the fastest routes through each region saves hours.

- **Use Mounts and Fast Travel:** Always fast travel when available.

- **Stack Speed Buffs:** Certain potions and gear increase movement speed.

4. Jack of All Trades Master All Character Classes in One Playthrough

Why It's Hard:

- Each class requires extensive skill points and time investment.

- Some skills are locked behind high-level content.

Pro Tips:

- **Plan Early:** Allocate skill points evenly across classes from the start.

- **Complete All Side Quests:** Side quests often grant skill points and rare gear.

- **Grind in High-Yield Areas:** Areas with frequent enemy spawns help with leveling.

- **Respec Wisely:** Use **Respec Tokens** (found in secret dungeons) to redistribute points.

5. Chicken Whisperer Survive the Chicken of Doom

Why It's Hard:

- The **Chicken of Doom** is a joke enemy with near-invincible stats.

- It can one-shot most players.

Pro Tips:

- **Trap It in the Environment:** Use narrow doorways to block its movement.

- **Use Environmental Hazards:** Lure it near traps and explosive barrels.

- **Use Ranged Attacks:** Keep your distance and whittle down its health.

- **Upgrade Your Gear:** Max-level weapons and armor are essential.

6. Eco-Friendly Finish the Game Without Using Health Potions

Why It's Hard:

- Health potions are a lifeline in tough battles.

- Requires excellent defensive play and efficient use of other healing methods.

Pro Tips:

- **Use Passive Healing Gear:** Certain armor pieces provide gradual health regeneration.

- **Stock Up on Food:** Consumables like cooked meals can restore health without violating the achievement.

- **Avoid Taking Damage:** Prioritize stealth and crowd control over direct combat.

- **Use Allies:** Summons and companion characters can draw aggro away from you.

Final Advice for Achievement Hunters:

- **Be Patient:** Difficult achievements require persistence. Don't get discouraged by failures.

- **Use Community Resources:** Forums and YouTube guides can offer valuable tips.

- **Play for Fun:** Achievements are rewarding, but the journey matters too.

Unlocking these challenging trophies is a testament to your skill and dedication. With the right strategy and perseverance, you can conquer every challenge *South of Midnight* has to offer.

Speedrunning and Completionist Goals

For players who crave mastery and efficiency, South of Midnight offers a thrilling playground for speedrunners and completionists alike. Whether you want to blaze through the game in record time or uncover every secret the world has to offer, this section outlines goals, strategies, and tips to help you achieve your objectives.

1. What is Speedrunning in South of Midnight?

Speedrunning involves completing the game as quickly as possible, often exploiting optimal routes, mechanics, and glitches (if allowed) to set record times. South of Midnight offers an official Speedrunner Mode, which includes an in-game timer and leaderboards for bragging rights.

Categories of Speedrunning:

Any% Completion: Finish the game as fast as possible, no matter how many quests or items you skip.

100% Completion: Complete all main and side quests, discover all collectibles, and fully explore every map.

No Major Glitches: A purist run where no game-breaking exploits are allowed.

Permadeath Speedrun: Complete the game on Permadeath Mode under a time limit without dying.

2. Speedrunning Tips and Strategies:

Route Optimization:

Memorize Fast Travel Points: Unlock and use Ethereal Shrines early to cut travel time.

Prioritize Mobility: Equip gear that increases movement speed and stamina recovery.

Skip Non-Essentials: Avoid combat unless necessary. Bosses and main objectives should be your focus.

Combat Efficiency:

Burst Damage Builds: Use high-damage weapons or magic to one-shot common enemies.

Utilize AoE (Area of Effect) Abilities: Defeating groups quickly saves time in required combat zones.

Item and Resource Management:

Stock Up Beforehand: Don't waste time gathering resources mid-run.
Use Consumables Wisely: Speed-boost potions and stamina recovery items are essential.

Save Time in Dialogue:

Skip Cutscenes: The game allows cutscene skipping in Speedrunner Mode.
Choose Fast Dialogue Options: Often, the shortest responses end conversations quickly.

3. Completionist Goals for Perfectionists

For players who want to experience every piece of content the game has to offer, completing South of Midnight to 100% is the ultimate challenge.

What Does 100% Completion Include?

- Completing the main storyline and all side quests.
- Defeating every boss (main, optional, and secret).
- Discovering all hidden locations and collectibles.
- Unlocking all weapons, armor, and cosmetic sets.
- Achieving every ending in the game.
- Completing the achievement and trophy list.

Checklist for Completionists:

- **Map Completion:** Uncover every region on the map.
- **Lore Collection:** Gather all journal entries, tomes, and NPC dialogue snippets.
- **Faction Reputation:** Max out your reputation with all three major factions.
- **Gear Mastery:** Collect and upgrade every weapon and armor set.
- **Secret Quests:** Complete hidden quests, like "Echoes of Eternity."
- **All Endings:** Unlock all five main endings and the secret ending.

4. Tools and Resources for Speedrunners and Completionists

Community Forums: Platforms like Speedrun.com and Reddit have forums where players share routes and tips.

YouTube Walkthroughs: Watch top players' runs to learn new strategies.

In-Game Tracker: South of Midnight features a completion percentage tracker to help you monitor progress.

Custom Save Slots: Use multiple save files to revisit key decision points.

Why Pursue Speedrunning or Completionist Goals?

Bragging Rights: Achieve leaderboard rankings or 100% completion bragging rights.

Sense of Achievement: Overcoming challenging goals provides immense satisfaction.

Unlock Exclusive Rewards: Some items and cosmetics are only accessible through full completion.

Join the Community: Share strategies and builds with fellow players.

Rewards and Special Unlocks

In *South of Midnight*, rewards go beyond simple loot drops. Special unlocks offer unique cosmetics, gameplay benefits, and bragging rights that keep players motivated to explore every corner of the game. This section covers the various categories of special unlocks and how to obtain them.

1. Cosmetic Rewards

Cosmetics in *South of Midnight* allow players to personalize their character's appearance, from armor skins to weapon designs.

Exclusive Skins:

- **Shadow Reaper Armor:**

  - o **How to Unlock:** Complete the game on **Permadeath Mode**.

- **Radiant Knight Set:**

  - o **How to Unlock:** Finish all main and side quests.

- **Golden Fang Bow:**

  - o **How to Unlock:** Achieve 100% map exploration.

Color Variants and Customization:

- Collect **Dyes of the Veil** scattered throughout the world to unlock armor color variations.

- Custom weapon ornaments are unlocked by completing faction loyalty quests.

2. Unique Weapons and Legendary Gear

Certain legendary weapons and gear offer both aesthetic appeal and gameplay advantages.

- **The Soulpiercer Blade:**

  - **Effect:** Lifesteal on hit.

  - **How to Unlock:** Defeat the secret boss **Eater of Stars** in under 5 minutes.

- **Veilbreaker Shield:**

  - **Effect:** Reflects 25% of damage back to enemies.

  - **How to Unlock:** Complete the **Trial of the Forgotten** with no deaths.

- **Lunar Crown Helm:**

  - **Effect:** Boosts experience gain by 20%.

  - **How to Unlock:** Collect every **Ancient Relic** in the game.

3. Achievement-Based Rewards

Certain achievements grant exclusive in-game perks.

- **Midnight Conqueror (Achievement):**

    o **Reward:** Grants the title **"Lord of Shadows"** and a glowing aura.

- **Speedrunner's Edge (Achievement):**

    o **Reward:** Unlocks a special mount called **The Ethereal Charger**.

- **Flawless Victor (Achievement):**

    o **Reward:** Exclusive **Phantom Blade** weapon skin.

4. Endgame Unlocks

After completing the main storyline, players gain access to special post-game content.

- **New Game+ Mode:**

    o Enemies are stronger, but gear progression continues.

- **Endless Dungeons:**

  o Procedurally generated dungeons with rare loot drops.

- **Faction Wars:**

  o Post-game faction conflicts offer repeatable quests with high-tier rewards.

5. Community Events and Seasonal Rewards

The developers of *South of Midnight* frequently host in-game events with exclusive, time-limited rewards.

- **Seasonal Events:**

  o Special holiday-themed quests that offer unique cosmetic items.

- **Leaderboard Challenges:**

  o Top-ranking players receive exclusive mounts and armor.

- **Twitch Drops:**

  o Watching official live streams can earn unique in-game items.

Why Chase These Rewards?

- **Bragging Rights:** Flaunt rare gear and titles in multiplayer modes.

- **Gameplay Advantages:** Legendary gear often provides significant stat boosts.

- **Replayability:** New Game+ and post-game content keep the experience fresh.

Whether you're racing against the clock or collecting every hidden item, *South of Midnight* offers countless opportunities to push your limits and reap satisfying rewards.

CHAPTER 10: ADVANCED TECHNIQUES AND ADDITIONAL RESOURCES

Pro-Level Gameplay Tips

For those aiming to master *South of Midnight*, it's not enough to just play you need to dominate. Pro-level gameplay involves strategic decision-making, precise execution, and understanding the game's deeper mechanics. Whether you're chasing leaderboard rankings or simply want to outperform the competition, these advanced tips will elevate your gameplay.

1. Mastering Combat Mechanics

Perfect Your Timing

- **Parrying is King:** The window for parrying in *South of Midnight* is tight, but the payoff is massive. Successful parries not only stagger enemies but also open them to critical hits.

- **Animation Cancelling:** Certain attacks can be interrupted with a dodge or ability, allowing faster follow-up attacks. Learn which animations can be canceled to maximize DPS.

Manage Stamina Wisely

- **Don't Overcommit:** Running out of stamina mid-fight can leave you vulnerable. Always reserve at least 20% stamina for emergency dodges.

- **Use Stamina Boosting Gear:** Rings and armor pieces with stamina regen perks ensure you can keep moving and attacking.

Mix Ranged and Melee Combat

- **Range for Control:** Use ranged attacks to bait out enemy abilities before closing the gap.

- **Close for the Kill:** Once an enemy's key abilities are on cooldown, switch to melee for the finishing blow.

2. Optimizing Character Builds

Know Your Playstyle:

- **Tank Build:** Prioritize health, armor, and taunt abilities to soak up damage in group play.

- **DPS Build:** Maximize critical hit chance and attack speed to dish out damage quickly.

- **Hybrid Build:** Combine moderate defense with strong offensive abilities for versatility.

Synergize Your Skills:

- Some abilities work better together. For example:

- Shadow Veil Cloak + Backstab: Go invisible, then strike for double damage.

- Lightning Pulse + Chain Reaction: Stun groups of enemies and deal AoE damage.

3. Exploiting Game Mechanics for Advantage

Environmental Awareness:

- **Use Terrain to Your Advantage:** Higher ground grants a damage boost for ranged attacks.

- **Environmental Hazards:** Lure enemies into traps, explosive barrels, or poisonous swamps.

Enemy Weakness Exploitation:

- **Scan for Vulnerabilities:** Some enemies are weak to specific elements or weapon types.

- **Boss Patterns:** Every boss has a "tell" before powerful attacks. Learning these patterns can turn a tough fight into an easy win.

4. Efficient Resource Management

Gold and Crafting Materials:

- **Don't Hoard Invest Wisely:** Upgrading one legendary weapon is better than having multiple under-leveled weapons.

- **Craft Instead of Buy:** Materials are abundant; use them to craft health potions, arrows, and traps instead of spending gold.

Consumable Strategy:

- **Health Potions:** Save high-tier health potions for boss fights.

- **Buff Potions:** Use attack and defense buffs before engaging elite enemies.

- **Overstacking is Key:** Carry more than you think you need it's better to be prepared.

5. PvP and Multiplayer Strategies

- **Play Mind Games:** In PvP, players often expect predictable behavior. Break the pattern with fake-outs and delayed attacks.

- **Use Cover and Terrain:** Stay unpredictable by constantly moving and using environmental cover.

- **Know When to Retreat:** In open-world PvP, disengaging and healing can give you a second chance to turn the tide.

6. Learn from the Best

- **Watch Top Players:** Analyze gameplay footage of top-ranked players to learn advanced strategies.

- **Join High-Level Guilds:** Being part of a guild with skilled players offers mentorship opportunities and insider tips.

- **Challenge Yourself:** Set personal challenges, like completing missions with unconventional builds, to improve adaptability.

Community Resources and Online Guides

No gamer becomes a master alone. The *South of Midnight* community is filled with passionate players, content creators, and forums that provide invaluable insights. Whether you need build suggestions, boss strategies, or just want to show off your achievements, these resources can enhance your gameplay experience.

1. Official Game Forums

The official **South of Midnight** forums are the best place to start. Players share tips, report bugs, and discuss game mechanics.

- **Forums Section:**

- Build Optimization: Community-sourced meta builds.

- Speedrunning Tips: Routes and time-saving techniques.

- Patch Notes & Updates: Stay informed on changes that might affect gameplay.

2. YouTube and Twitch Channels

Top Content Creators:

- **MidnightMastery:** Known for deep-dive builds and speedrun strategies.

- **ShadowWarden:** Specializes in PvP tactics and high-level boss battles.

- **LoreHunterTV:** Explores hidden secrets, Easter eggs, and lore theories.

Why Watch Streamers?

- **Learn New Strategies:** Watching live gameplay helps you see how experts handle tough encounters.

- **Stay Updated:** Streamers often get early access to patches and DLCs.

- **Engage with the Community:** Twitch chats and YouTube comments can be a goldmine for tips.

3. Community Forums and Social Platforms

Reddit (r/SouthOfMidnight):

- Active community with build discussions, fan art, and tips for newcomers.

- Weekly challenge threads to keep gameplay fresh.

Discord Servers:

- Real-time help with bosses, build advice, and matchmaking for multiplayer content.

- Join guilds and find dedicated raid teams.

4. Fan-Made Guides and Wikis

- **Midnight Codex (Wiki):**

  - Complete breakdown of items, locations, and lore.

- **Midnight Tools:**

  - Build calculators, damage optimizers, and item drop trackers.

- **Speedrun.com:**

  - Track record times and learn the fastest routes.

5. Online Marketplaces and Trading Hubs

- **Marketplace Forums:**

  - Trade legendary weapons, armor sets, and rare crafting materials.

- **In-Game Economy Tips:**

  - Learn how to profit from rare item farming and trade flipping.

Why Engage with the Community?

- **Stay Ahead of the Curve:** Community members often discover exploits, hidden quests, or optimal builds before official guides are updated.

- **Make Friends and Collaborate:** Guilds and clans provide not only gameplay benefits but also a sense of community.

- **Get Real-Time Help:** Stuck on a boss? Post a question and get immediate feedback.

Leveraging the wisdom of the community and honing pro-level gameplay skills will make *South of Midnight* more than just a game it will become your playground. From mastering combat mechanics to networking with fellow players, there are countless ways to keep improving. Embrace the challenge, join the community, and carve your name in the annals of *South of Midnight* legends.

Mods and Customization Options

One of the most exciting aspects of *South of Midnight* is its modding community and the variety of customization options available to players. Whether you're looking to enhance graphics, tweak gameplay mechanics, or add entirely new content, mods allow you to personalize your experience. This section explores the best mods, how to install them safely, and the in-game customization features that let you tailor the world to your liking.

1. The Role of Mods in South of Midnight

Mods, or modifications, are player-created files that alter the game in various ways. The *South of Midnight* community has embraced modding to improve visuals, adjust mechanics, and expand gameplay content.

Why Use Mods?

- **Enhanced Visuals:** Higher resolution textures, lighting adjustments, and improved character models.

- **Gameplay Tweaks:** Adjust difficulty, enemy AI, or inventory limits.

- **New Content:** Custom quests, weapons, and even entire regions.

- **Quality of Life (QoL):** Faster inventory management, better UI readability, or quicker crafting.

2. Popular Mods and Their Benefits

Graphics Overhaul Mods:

- **Midnight ReShade:** Improves lighting, shadows, and overall color palette for a more immersive experience.

- **4K Texture Pack:** Upscales textures on characters, environments, and gear.

Gameplay Mods:

- **No Stamina Drain:** Removes or reduces stamina consumption for faster-paced combat.

- **Enhanced Enemy AI:** Makes enemies more unpredictable and challenging.

- **Level Cap Remover:** Allows progression beyond the base level cap.

Customization Mods:

- **Armor Dye Expansion:** Unlocks additional colors and patterns for all armor sets.

- **Custom Character Creator:** Adds new hairstyles, tattoos, and facial features.

Fun and Whimsical Mods:

- **Big Head Mode:** A nostalgic nod to classic games, making character heads hilariously oversized.

- **Pet Companions:** Adds dogs, cats, or mythical creatures to accompany players.

3. How to Safely Install Mods

Step-by-Step Installation Guide:

1. **Backup Your Saves:** Always back up your game data before installing mods.

2. **Use Trusted Mod Platforms:**

   o **Nexus Mods:** The most reputable source for safe and tested mods.

   o **Steam Workshop (if available):** Integrated and secure.

3. **Download a Mod Manager:**

   o **Vortex** or **Mod Organizer 2** makes installation easier and helps manage load orders.

4. **Check for Compatibility:**

   o Ensure mods are compatible with your game
      version.

   o Read user comments for bug reports.

5. **Test After Installation:**

   o Load the game after installing each mod to
      troubleshoot issues early.

4. In-Game Customization Options

Even without mods, *South of Midnight* offers robust customization
options that let players tweak their experience:

HUD and Interface Adjustments:

- **Toggle HUD Elements:** Hide the minimap, health bar, or
  quest markers for an immersive experience.

- **Resizable UI:** Customize text size and interface placement.

Difficulty Settings:

- Adjust difficulty on the fly, from **Story Mode** to **Nightmare
  Mode**, depending on the challenge you seek.

Cosmetic Customization:

- **Character Appearance:** Change hairstyles, tattoos, and outfits at any time via the in-game **Appearance Mirrors**.

- **Mounts and Companions:** Unlock different skins and accessories for your mounts and pets.

5. Cautionary Notes on Modding

- **Risk of Corruption:** Some mods may corrupt save files if improperly installed.

- **Disable Before Updates:** Always disable mods before applying game patches to avoid conflicts.

- **Beware of Cheats:** Some mods offer cheats that may void achievements or lead to account bans in multiplayer.

Future Updates and DLC Content

The journey through *South of Midnight* doesn't end with the base game. The developers have committed to an exciting post-launch roadmap that includes free updates, seasonal events, and expansive DLCs. This section outlines what players can look forward to and how upcoming content will enhance the game.

1. Developer Roadmap and Promised Updates

The developers of *South of Midnight* have released a detailed roadmap outlining the game's future.

Upcoming Free Updates:

- **QoL Patch 1.1:** Improved load times, UI adjustments, and bug fixes.

- **New Game+ Mode:** Carry over gear and abilities for a tougher replay experience.

- **Seasonal Events:** Special events tied to in-game lore with unique rewards.

2. Major DLC Expansions

The developers have announced two major DLCs that will expand the lore and gameplay experience.

DLC 1: The Veil of Eternity

- **Release Date:** Q2 of next year.

- **Plot:** Explores the shadowy realm beyond the living world.

- **New Features:**

- New Region: Vast open-world areas with dynamic weather.

- New Bosses: Five powerful entities tied to the realm of shadows.

- New Abilities: Shadow-based magic for stealth and crowd control.

DLC 2: Wrath of the Lost Gods

- **Release Date:** End of the year.

- **Plot:** Centers around a rebellion of forgotten deities seeking to reclaim the world.

- **New Features:**

    - **Playable Deity Forms:** Temporarily take the form of powerful gods.

    - **Mythical Weapons:** Collect divine weapons with game-changing abilities.

    - **Faction Wars:** Align with different gods for unique rewards.

3. Seasonal Events and Limited-Time Content

Seasonal events add a dynamic element to the game with exclusive, time-limited content.

Examples of Seasonal Events:

- **Midnight Harvest:** A Halloween-themed event where players hunt spectral creatures.

- **Festival of Lights:** A winter event with festive cosmetics and community challenges.

- **Faction Rally:** Compete in faction-based PvP events with rotating rewards.

4. Community Involvement in Future Content

The developers actively engage with the community to shape future updates.

- **Player Polls:** Fans vote on which features or cosmetics they want next.

- **Feedback Forums:** Regular feedback threads help prioritize bug fixes and content adjustments.

- **Modder Collaborations:** Some community mods have been officially integrated into the game.

5. How to Stay Updated on New Content

- **Follow Official Channels:**

    - Twitter, Discord, and the official website provide real-time updates.

- **Join the Community:**

    - Reddit and forums often leak content or share early impressions.

- **Subscribe to Newsletters:**

    - Get exclusive insights, early access offers, and event reminders.

Final Thoughts:

The future of *South of Midnight* looks bright, with a steady stream of updates and expansions designed to keep the game fresh and engaging. Whether you're eager for new storylines, challenging bosses, or simply more customization options, there's something on the horizon for everyone. Stay tuned, stay engaged, and continue to explore the mysterious world *South of Midnight* has to offer.